W9-BJA-409

MICKEY
MANTLE

Memories of MICKEY MANTLE

My very best friend

MARSHALL SMITH
& John Rohde

ADVENTURE
QUEST
INC.

COPYRIGHT 1996
ADVENTURE QUEST INC

Copyright © 1996 by

ADVENTURE QUEST, INC.

25 Park View Avenue

Bronxville, NY 10708

All rights reserved. No part of this publication may be reproduced, stored in a retrieval system or transmitted in any form or by any electronic, mechanical, photocopying or otherwise, without written permission of the copyright owner.

FIRST EDITION PUBLISHED IN 1996 BY

ADVENTURE QUEST, INC.

BRONXVILLE, NY 10708

Library of Congress Cataloging in Publication Data

PRINTED IN THE USA

BY JOSTENS PRINTING AND PUBLISHING

FIRST EDITION

10-9-8-7-6-5-4-3-2-1

ISBN 1-888170-01-8

All worldwide rights reserved by Adventure Quest, Inc.

Table of Contents

FOREWORD PAGE 2

THE DIAGNOSIS 12

MEETING THE MICK 26

TEE TIME 54

LEAVING THE SCENE 84

REMEMBER WHEN - MICKEY'S SCRAPBOOK 108

HERE COMES THE BRIDE 154

SIGN HERE PLEASE 166

LOSING A LEGEND 186

EULOGY 202

ACKNOWLEDGMENTS

The research and compilation for a publication of this magnitude requires the tremendous effort and assistance of a large number of people. Fortunately Adventure Quest, Inc. can boast such a dedicated group of professionals. That special photograph or piece of memorabilia rarely seen by others, but uncovered because of the extra effort put forth by this group, has greatly contributed to the uniqueness of this book.

Now, as we celebrate a friendship of two very special individuals, we should also acknowledge those people who have allowed us to enjoy and cherish rekindled memories of a special time and hero.

First and foremost, I would like to thank Marshall Smith, a true golf "teacher" and personality extraordinaire for sharing with us almost fifty years of his life and friendship with Mickey Mantle. Also John Rhode, a "Diamond in the Rough," who will soon be recognized for his many gifts and talents as a writer and publisher's dream. I also greatly appreciate the assistance of Corinne Smith who handled most of the photo research and collection, without whom this task would not have been completed. The editorial staff headed by Elizabeth (Betsy) Girard and assisted by Frank Casaccio and Maribeth Waddell did an outstanding job under less than perfect conditions. Jim Toomey, Ron Ramsey, Greg Mosier and Ted Watts shared their many creative talents in the design, organization and professional quality of this book. I'd especially like to thank Sandy Hayes for keeping all our spirits up and our sense of self importance in check. Tom Catal and Andy Vilacky added their charm and their Mickey Mantle photo collections. Finally, to Jan Russo, a special thanks for a job well done.

The Publisher.

Book Production

Elizabeth A. Girard
Senior Editor

Frank Casaccio
Assistant Editor

Maribeth Waddell
Assistant Editor

Book Design
James Toomey

Art Director
Ron Ramsey

Jacket Art
Ted Watts

Jacket Title
Greg Mosier

T e s t i m o n i a l s

WALT ZEMBRISKI

"Marshall Smith and I have been friends since 1986 when we met on the practice range. He was giving a lesson to Chi Chi Rodriguez, when I walked up and said 'who are you?' When he told me I said, 'I could use some help with my short game.' He gave me some lessons and I won three tournaments. He has been a good friend ever since."

BOBBY MURCER

"I have known Marshall for over 25 years and I have never had a more loyal friend. He epitomizes that Oklahoma drawl and is someone you can always count on to get the job done."

HANK BAUER

"Marshall Smith has been my friend and I hope he will be for years to come. He truly was Mickey's very best friend."

MOOSE SKOWRON

"We have been friends since Joplin, Missouri, when Marshall first proposed the Mickey Mantle Tournament and we have been the best of friends ever since. He does one heck of a job with anything he attempts."

DARRELL ROYAL

"I've known Marshall for over 25 years, and every time our paths cross it's fun all over again. He knows he can always call on me and I know I can always call on him."

BILL GRIGSBY - Broadcaster of Major League Baseball and NFL Football

"Marshall Smith is 'Home Town.' His laid-back, charismatic style puts a person at ease - whether on the practice tee for a lesson or over a refresher on the nineteenth hole. Marshall is the kind of person Mickey felt comfortable with. He could trust him and he could learn from him. The only contract ever needed with Marshall is a handshake. His book is a winner."

DICK LYNCH

"Marshall Smith makes life and the game of golf fun. His friendship with Mickey was truly a joy to behold. Two men with similar backgrounds became giants in their chosen professions."

STEVE OWEN - Athletic Director, The University of Oklahoma

"This is about enduring friendship. I have known Marshall Smith for over twenty-five years. He has given me golf lessons, advice, wisdom from his life experience... and the thrill of getting to know the great Mickey Mantle. Theirs was a special bond, passing the test of time. I am proud to call Marshall Smith my friend."

CHI CHI RODRIGUEZ - Pro Golfer

"Marshall Smith is a great golfer, instructor and close friend. I look forward to reading his book on Mickey."

WALTER E. NEULS - President and Chm. of Board Colonial Casualty Ins. Co.

"Marshall Smith is my (very) best friend. Unfortunately I have to share that friendship with every other person he knows or has ever met. Spend 10 minutes with him and you will be treated as though you have known each other for a lifetime."

DEDICATION

To Corinne, my wife, thanks for putting up with Mickey and me for all those years.

To Mickey, my friend, thanks for the memories of all those years.

"If there were only two men in the world, how would they get on? They would help one another, harm one another, flatter one another, slander one another, fight one another, and make it up, they could neither live together nor do without one another."

- VOLTAIRE

FOREWORD

T his is not a book about baseball. This is a book about friendship. For nearly half a century, Marshall Smith befriended Mickey Mantle, a blue-eyed blond from Oklahoma who just happened to become the most powerful switch-hitter in the history of major league baseball.

There were: 536 career home runs; a .298 lifetime batting average; a record 2,041 games as a Yankee; 1,734 walks; 1,710 strikeouts; 16 All-Star games; 12 American League pennants; seven World Series rings; three Most Valuable Player awards; the magical year of 1956 that included the Triple Crown, Hickock Belt and Silver Bat; and the Gold Glove in 1962.

Fans knew Mickey Mantle by the numbers.

Marshall Smith knew Mickey Mantle by the heart.

Books about Mantle have been written and rewritten. Naturally, because Mantle was who he was, baseball often will be used as a point of ref-

Mickey Mantle and Marshall Smith during the early years.

erence in the upcoming pages -- from the time Mantle played in the Ban Johnson League, to signing with the New York Yankees, to joining their Class D farm club in the K-O-M (Kansas-Oklahoma-Missouri) League at Independence, Kan., to Class C ball in Joplin, Mo., to playing for the Yankees, to being sent down to Triple-A ball in Kansas City, to being called back up to the Yankees seven weeks later. He accomplished all this by age 19.

Mantle fans habitually related occurrences in their lives to occurrences in his. Mantle's life was firmly embedded in their brains. They lived vicariously through his displays of resounding courage, remarkable athleticism and relentless determination. Their highs and lows changed when his changed, which was frequently.

Smith's knowledge of the man was far more in-depth than pages in the Baseball Encyclopedia. "When he limped, I limped," Smith said. "When he ached, I ached."

And Mantle ached plenty. There were the

Mickey standing under his street sign in Commerce, Oklahoma. Photo taken by Marshall Smith in Oct. 1994.

knee injuries, the foot injuries, the torn hamstrings, the damaged shoulders, not to mention a battle against osteomyelitis, an infectious inflammatory disease of the bone. When Mantle was 14, one doctor suggested amputating one of his legs. Mantle's mother, Lovell, nixed the idea.

Was Mantle the greatest ever to play the game? That's debatable.

Was he the greatest cripple ever to play the game? No contest.

Smith first met Mantle while playing for an opposing football team in high school. From there the association grew, with a brief stint as a basketball teammate, to a long stint with golf, to a lifetime of friendship. Their bond was closest in the end.

"He was my very best friend," Smith will tell you repeatedly.

A section of the Smith household in Miami, Okla., resembles a museum, adorned with what Smith humbly refers to as "memorabilities." There are sketches, posters and paintings of his very best

Self Portrait taken in Marshall Smith's car in September 1994.

friend. There are books, videotapes, magazines and newspaper articles. There are hats, T-shirts, jackets, golf balls, tees, ball markers, pens, pencils and money clips adorned with Mantle's name. And there are photographs, stacks of photographs. Rather than install a turnstile and charge admission, Marshall and his wife, Corinne, gladly share their memories with friends and neighbors. No "For Sale" is attached to a single item. "That would be dirty," Corinne explained.

Smith, a former Class A club pro, taught Mantle how to play golf. For the final 40 years of his life, when not playing baseball or signing autographs, Mantle was obsessed by golf. "I was extremely fortunate," said Smith, who was five years older than Mantle. "Through Mickey, I was able to meet so many wonderful people and we were able to visit various golf courses around the country. We just absolutely had a ball all the time."

Throughout the 1950s, perhaps no athlete was photographed more often than Mantle, who grew up in Commerce, a town in the heart of lead and

Baxter Springs, Kansas baseball field where Mickey hit three home runs during one game in the summer of 1948.

zinc country in the far northeast corner of Oklahoma. (Forty years later came a dead-ringer look-alike in Dallas Cowboys quarterback Troy Aikman, who played his high school ball in Henryetta, Okla., some 150 miles to the southwest.)

Smith and Mantle often took pictures while driving around their old neighborhoods. They went to places named Miami, Commerce, Jay, Vinita, Grove, Spavinaw, Quapaw, Picher and Cardin. Some of them barely qualify for post offices. "They're just sort of ... there," Smith explained. Other towns such as Whitebird, Douthat, Zincville, Lincolnville and Hockerville existed back then, but not now.

Mantle was born in Spavinaw on Oct. 20, 1931, and moved roughly 40 miles north to Commerce when he was 4. In what would be one of Mantle's final trips to the Commerce area, he and Smith stopped at various landmarks that rekindled old memories. Mantle posed by a street sign bearing the name Mickey Mantle Blvd. He stood outside a pint-sized house he used to call home at 319 South Quincy Street. The best picture that day was one Mantle took of himself while riding in the passenger's side of Smith's car.

Mantle's father, Elven Clark Mantle, was nicknamed "Mutt."

Marshall McLemore Smith was nicknamed 'Mott."

Mickey poses with five Playboy centerfolds during a promotional tour in Miami Florida; October 1980.

Grown men named Mutt and Mott occupied Mantle's entire lifetime.

"Somebody always has to have somebody to confide in," Smith said. "We confided in each other. Mickey and I always shot square with one another."

Parts of Mantle's life resembled fantasy. There also was pain and suffering. Some of the pain was unavoidable. Some was self-inflicted. The Mantle legend was mythical, surreal, fascinating, incredibly romantic and, during its low points, disgustingly pathetic. His life was one big tragicomedy.

Books depicting Mantle's history vary slightly. Names, dates and sites don't jibe. Circumstances are described differently. Where Mickey lived and when. What Mickey did and when. Whether he hit two home runs or three, and

how far each traveled. Some of this was produced by Mantle himself, who often spiced up stories to add flavor. But his fiction had all the kick of parsley. The embellishments were harmless, yet a source of frustration for Smith. "He always told people about that football game in high school," Smith recalled. "He'd tell everybody that his team killed us. I think the last time he told the story the final score was something like 47-0. So I pulled out a yearbook and looked it up. They beat us 6-0. Mickey looked at me and just said, 'Nah, that book's not right.' "

An often-told story occurred in the summer of 1948, prior to Mantle's senior year at Commerce High School when he played in a Ban Johnson League game at Baxter Springs, Kan. He was a hard-hitting, wild-throwing shortstop on a team known as the "Whiz Kids." The park's outer boundary was the Spring River, which flowed diagonally across a low-lying field. In right field, the front bank of the water hazard was roughly 500 feet from home plate. Center field extended to about 400 feet and left field was approximately 450 feet. In 1948, with an overflow crowd of 200-300 looking on, Mantle launched three home runs (two right-handed and one left-handed, according to Mantle; two left-handed and one right-handed, according to another source; a night game, according to Mantle; an afternoon game, according to someone else).

The first blow, to right-center, was said to

have bounced once before finding the river. The second blow also was to right-center, only deeper. The final blow was a towering shot to center field that landed in the stream. The awe-inspired crowd was so impressed, a straw hat was passed throughout the stands in appreciation for what this shy 16-year-old Okie had just done. When the hat came to rest, inside was $53 (or $54, take your pick) in small change waiting for Mantle.

Through the years, the dollar amount has remained roughly the same. Distances of the home runs, however, have lengthened considerably. "The first time Mick told me that story, he said the balls found the river on one hop," Smith said. "Then they went into the river on the fly. Then they all cleared the river, which is impossible (a minimum clout of roughly 700 feet to straight-away center would be required). But that was Mickey. I had to put up with that kind of stuff all the time."

Several months after Mantle's death on Aug. 13, 1995, Smith still struggled with acceptance. Particularly painful was watching a videotape of Mantle's candid interview with NBC's Bob Costas in March of 1994. In it, a red-eyed Mantle discussed his month-long stay at the Betty Ford Center for alcohol abuse. "Maybe I do, in the back of my mind, feel like I've let everybody down in some way or another," Mantle told Costas. "I hope people in the end will say, 'He turned out all right. I'm proud that I named my son Mickey.' That would be nice."

Mantle's eyes teared up. So, too, did the eyes of Smith, who walked outside into a steady Oklahoma wind for some fresh air. A few minutes later, Smith stepped back inside. "Whew," he said, wiping his tears. "Every time I watch that damn thing it gets to me. Lord, I miss him."

Smith knew who Mantle was. However, there were more than a few times Mantle didn't know who Mantle was. "The thing I remember most about him is he didn't realize he was Mickey Mantle," Smith said. "Being thought of as a legend just wasn't all that important to him. He didn't understand what all the fuss was about."

What follows in this book are a few examples of "all the fuss."

The purpose of this book is not to embarrass Mickey Mantle. Nor is it to ridicule, degrade or canonize the man. The purpose here is to simply share him. No disrespect is intended toward his wife, Merlyn, or the Mantle family. "Merlyn and the kids always treated me great," Smith said. "I always had a place to stay at Mickey's house in Dallas at 5730 Watson Circle. I was treated warmly. I think Merlyn loved Mickey to play golf with me because she knew he was in good hands."

There are a million Mickey Mantle stories. Some might actually be true. Smith has heard more than his share. He also has seen more than his share -- the battles with autograph hounds and with alcohol; the public Mantle as opposed to the private Mantle; the good times and the bad; the

Mickey standing in front of the house where he grew up in Commerce, Oklahoma; October 1994.

pain-free and painful; the womanizing.

"Oh, gosh," Smith said with a mischievous smile. "Boy, I could tell you stories ... I used to think Mickey could fill the Coleman (an historical theater in Miami) with all his women. Now I think he could have filled Yankee Stadium."

There are potential R-rated ventures about Mantle waiting to be written. This particular venture has a hint of PG-13, but overall is rated G. General audiences permitted.

"Mickey once told me, 'Please don't write a book about me before I die. You know more about me than anybody,' " Smith said.

Smith views his friendships on a color-bar scheme. "True-blue" gets the highest rating. And if you were "needled," well, that was the ultimate.

"Most of Mickey's friends were sort of hollow," Smith said. "They always seemed to want something from him. But he was true-blue. I didn't know anyone better. If you were a true friend of Mickey's, you were a friend for life. He didn't have a lot of true-blue friends. He had a few friends in baseball like Hank (Bauer), Billy (Martin), Whitey (Ford), Moose (Skowron) and Yogi (Berra). A few like that, but not many. Mickey would never let anybody get too close to him without going through me first. It was kind of like a screening process. He did the same for me. He'd say, 'Marshall, that might be a friend of yours, but I don't like him.'

"Mickey taught me when they put the needle in you, that means they love you. You're a friend. If they don't put the needle in you, well, you're just somebody else. I'll always remember that because I used to ask him, 'Why do you put the needle in me so much, Mickey?' He said, 'Because I love ya. That's the finest compliment I know how to pay you.' "

Mantle dedicated his autobiography *The Mick* to his fans. "This book is for you," Mantle stated. "I hope I got it right."

Marshall Smith dedicates this book to his very best friend, Mickey Mantle.

"I hope I got it right, too," Smith said.

THE DIAGNOSIS

In early September of 1994, Mickey Mantle and longtime friend Marshall Smith were at one of their favorite places -- the Shangri-La Resort in northeast Oklahoma. There, on Grand Lake O' the Cherokees, they could eat, golf, fish and relax. Not necessarily in that order.

During this particular relaxation period, Mantle and Smith were discussing baseball legend Stan Musial and golfer Chi Chi Rodriguez and their recent bouts with prostate cancer. An alarm went off in Mantle's head.

"You know what, I haven't had a complete physical since the last time I visited the Mayo," Mantle told Smith.

"I've never had a complete physical," Smith told Mantle.

It had been 28 years since Mantle had been to the Mayo Clinic in Rochester, Minn., where he underwent shoulder surgery prior to the 1966 season. But 1994 had been his healthiest year

Mickey doffs his hat to reporters at a news conference following his liver transplant at Baylor University Medical Center, Dallas, Texas; July 1995.

The post card Mickey would sign and hand out to autograph seekers.

since Lord knows when. Retirement, loneliness, various failed business ventures, autograph shows and hero worship had consumed Mantle's life the previous 25 years. His pain reliever of choice had been alcohol.

At the pleading of some close friends -- youngest son Danny, Pat Summerall, Whitey Ford, girlfriend Greer Johnson and Smith -- Mantle dug in, swung hard and decided to do all he could to swat this alcohol problem out of the park.

It was a vintage Mantle at-bat. All or nothing.

In late December of 1993, after being told his next drink might be his last, Mantle checked into the Betty Ford Center for a 30-day rehabilitation.

Mantle shared the following story:

A couple of days after checking in, he wasn't convinced this particular program was for him. He promptly called a cab.

Cabbie: "Where to, Mac?"

Mantle: "Actually, it's Mick. And take me to the nearest bar."

Mantle purchased a beer, placed it in front of him and stared at it. Stared at it for a good 30 minutes, never taking a sip. He left the beer intact and again called a cab.

Cabbie: "Where to, Mick?"

Mantle: "Back to that damn clinic."

Mantle and Smith were instructed to take two laxatives and have nothing but liquids for dinner the night before.

"I think that's a terrific story," Smith said. "That shows he was on his way to recovery. After he got out, other than water or Diet Coke, the only thing I saw him drink was (the non-alcoholic beer) O'Doul's."

Not even the death of one of his four sons, Billy, in March of 1994 could detour Mantle's determined journey to sobriety. "He felt great, better than he felt in years," Smith said. "He just wanted to have a check-up."

Mantle had done charity work with the Warren Foundation in Tulsa. Smith, a popular golf instructor in the area, started calling doctors who had doubled as his golfing buddies, looking for suggestions. A thorough examination for both men was scheduled for 8 a.m. on Sept. 12. Mantle and Smith were instructed to take two laxatives and have nothing but liquids for dinner the night before. At 6 a.m. the next day, they were to take one plain Fleet enema before going to the medical center.

On their 95-mile trek to Tulsa the day before the exam, Mantle and Smith stopped at a Wal-Mart in Grove, Oklahoma. Walking up and down the isle, looking for laxatives and an enema, was a befuddled 62-year-old Hall of Famer who had crushed some of the longest home runs in major league history.

Smith, who had been waiting in the car for roughly 20 minutes, walked into the store and found Mantle flanked by two elderly ladies, one tucked under each arm. "They were helping him look for what he needed. It was funny as hell," Smith explained. "Neither one of them knew it was Mickey Mantle, but word started getting around."

Within minutes, the enema man was surrounded by autograph hounds. Smith knew precisely what to do. He went back to Mantle's car, pulled out a fistful of autographed cards Mantle kept for such emergencies, and began handing them out to the gawkers.

Staying at a hotel near the Warren Medical Center, Mantle and Smith had their liquid dinners. A year earlier, Mantle's liquid entree would have consisted of red wine, vodka, a more powerful concoction, or all of the above. But this was his ninth month of sobriety. He hadn't had a drop of booze all year. Mantle hadn't been this sober since he first played baseball for the Yankees at age 19.

After an uncomfortable night, Mantle and Smith awoke inside their adjoining hotel rooms. Neither had ever had the displeasure of giving himself an enema before. Smith entered Mantle's room.

Smith (naked): "Hey, Mick. How do I do this?"

*T*he person diagnosed as being more healthy won $100 from the other guy

Mantle (naked): "I'm not sure. But let me tell you this, you'll do yours and I'll do mine. Now get the hell out of here."

Mantle and Smith truly were close. "Yeah, but we weren't that close," Smith said shaking his head.

Prior to the 2 1/2-day exam, Mantle and Smith did something they often did. They wagered. The person diagnosed as being more healthy won $100 from the other guy.

Heading the diagnostic team of roughly a dozen physicians was Dr. J. Frederick McNeer (internal medicine-cardiovascular disease), a man Mantle had never met. McNeer was a huge fan. He had seen Mantle hit a 515-foot home run directly over his head deep into the right-field bleachers when McNeer was an 11-year-old watching the Yankees play the White Sox at Comiskey Park in 1957.

"He was like Roy Hobbs (a fictitious baseball hero portrayed by Robert Redford in the movie 'The Natural')," McNeer said. "Only Mickey was better."

Mantle charmed McNeer with baseball memories. "He was filled with stories," McNeer said. "You just wanted to sit there and let him talk."

Before Mantle left, he asked one of the dozen physicians if he could have a shot to help increase his, uh, potency. Mantle received the shot and telephoned Smith four days later.

Mantle: "You've got to get ahold of that doctor."

Smith: "Why? What's wrong?"

Mantle: "That shot he gave me doesn't work."

Smith: "He said it wouldn't work right away, Mick. You've got to give it at least two weeks."

Two weeks and one day later, Mantle again called Smith.

Mantle: "I would prescribe this for anybody. It's working fine. This is just great!"

As it turned out, Smith needed a biopsy from the exam (which was benign) and lost the $100 bet. "I paid him right away," Smith assured. "Whoever lost always paid right there on the spot."

Sadly, Smith had paid his debt too soon.

On Sept. 23, McNeer sent a six-page letter to Mantle at his 6070 Break Point Trail address in Dallas.

The lab profile began with good news. Mantle's total cholesterol was excellent (129). The complete blood type found no evidence of anemia or nutritional deficiency, which meant there was no type of cancer-leukemia or lymphoma/Hodgkin's disease.

Hodgkin's had affected generations of Mantle men. There's a saying, "Deaths come in threes." For Mickey Mantle, deaths came in fives.

His grandfather, Charlie, died of the disease in 1944 when Mantle was 12. "Grandpa suddenly became old and feeble, almost overnight," Mantle said in *The Mick*, his third autobiography. "He died shortly after we moved (away from Commerce). I never forgot that moment, standing beside the casket with my little twin brothers Ray and Roy, the three of us looking down on him, and my father whispering, 'Say good-bye to Grandpa ...' "

"Mickey was always a sensitive person," cousin Ron Mantle once said. "He was that way his whole life. He was always the first one who would cry. He laughed a lot. Everything good or bad that ever happened in his life, if you knew Mick, he cried over. Me, I'm the cold one, but Mick was something else."

In 1947, uncle Eugene "Tunny" Mantle died at age 34, going from 215 pounds to 90 pounds in roughly 18 months. Another uncle, Emmett, died of the disease at age 32. On May 6, 1952, Mantle's father, Mutt, died less than two months after his 40th birthday. And two generations later, Billy Mantle was diagnosed with Hodgkin's at age 19. He eventually had major heart surgery, battled alcohol and drug problems, then died of a heart attack at age 36 in March of 1994.

"It made me wonder about what was out there (in the Commerce area)," McNeer said, trying to explain the ugly pattern within the Mantle men. "You hear it supposedly came from working the mines, but Billy didn't work in the mines. You wonder if it was something environmental. You can treat Hodgkin's now, but it's very unlikely that, back then, you could have a treatment."

Mickey had overcome the Mantle curse. However, bad news came near the bottom of page 3 in the lab profile.

"While there was no evidence for Type A or Type B hepatitis, there was evidence for exposure to Type C hepatitis," McNeer wrote. "The Type C virus is one that can be associated with slow but progressive inflammation of the liver which can result in scarring and damage (cirrhosis)."

McNeer went on to inform Mantle there was no direct relation to alcohol and Type C hepatitis. "You can have hepatitis C and never have had a drink in your life," McNeer explained after Mantle's death. "That has nothing to do with alcohol. That's an independent analysis. There are plenty of alcoholics who don't have hepatitis C. I kept telling him, 'You can get this even if you're not drinking.' But it (Type C) will ruin your liver and still be a significant risk for primary liver cancer, which Mickey had. It doesn't necessarily have anything to do with bad living habits. Certainly in the last few months, Mickey had been living an exemplary life. He didn't drink, he didn't do drugs, and he didn't smoke."

On the front page of McNeer's profile, in big type, was a list of five specialists he categorized as the "Mickey Mantles" of Type C hepatitis evalua-

> **"If he hadn't had hepatitis C, there's no telling how long he would have lived.**

tion. In McNeer's opinion, these were the best -- Dr. Willis Madry of Southwestern Medical Center in Dallas; Dr. Jeffrey Crippin of Baylor University Medical Center in Dallas; Dr. Russell Weisner of the Mayo Clinic in Rochester, Minn.; Dr. Eugene Schiff of the University of Miami Medical Center; and Dr. David M. Van Thiel of Baptist Medical Center in Oklahoma City.

McNeer had tried his best to simplify the complex diagnosis. "It was in 'doctorese,' because we talk our own language," McNeer said of his letter to Mantle. "We try to communicate as best we can, but sometimes people have a limited understanding, or catch bits and pieces of what we're talking about. He was a great athlete, but he was a lot like most of us. He just didn't understand medicine."

Other than the hepatitis C -- and it's impossible to ignore such a deadly disease -- Mantle's overall health was good.

"When I first saw him, his muscle tone was incredible for a 62-year-old man," McNeer said. "He said none of his body parts worked. Well, he was exaggerating. Everything but his liver worked. He was being a little bit humble when he compared everything to his liver. Hepatitis is inflamation of the liver. A great percentage of those people will go on and develop a permanent liver tumor. That's what happened with Mickey. The tumor was picked up, unfortunately, a little too late. If they had gotten it all out (similar to the operation with actor Larry Hagman), Mickey might still be alive. He was a very strong man. If he hadn't had hepatitis C, there's no telling how long he would have lived."

If Mantle didn't get hepatitis C from drinking to excess, where did he get it? Was it all those cortisone shots he had taken to combat the constant pain throughout his career? Or was it the disastrous flu shot he took in early September of 1961 while he was involved in a captivating game of Home Run Derby against teammate Roger Maris?

Battling a nagging head cold, Mantle took the advice of longtime Yankees' broadcaster, Mel Allen. Allen set up an appointment with Dr. Max Jacobson. Often referred to as "Dr. Feel Good," Jacobson's patients included Elizabeth Taylor, Eddie Fisher, Tennessee Williams and President John F. Kennedy, for whom Jacobson prescribed hefty doses of Demerol to relieve the commander-in-chief's various physical ailments.

"He (Jacobson) greets me at the door wearing a white smock with bloodstains all over it," Mantle explained. "Like a lamb, I follow him into his office. Now I'm watching him prepare a syringe and needle. He's mixing the stuff and so help me his eyes are literally rolling in his head as he draws a smoky liquid from the vial, squirts a little in the air, and tells me to pull down my pants. I oblige. He walks around. 'All right, here we go. This might hurt, but then again it might not.' As soon as he hits the skin, I scream. 'Goddamn, that hurts!' He stuck the needle up too high. It felt as though he had stuck a red-hot poker into me. I'm paralyzed. He slaps me on the back. 'Walk back to the hotel. Don't take a cab, you'll be fine.' "

Mantle ended up in New York City's Lenox Hill Hospital, where they lanced the wound, cutting a three-inch scar over the hip bone, allowing it to drain. "It left a hole so big that you could put a golf ball in it," Mantle said. "P.S. The Yankee front office was furious. P.P.S. Dr. Max sent me a bill. I never did pay it. I wanted to sue him. A few years later he stopped practicing."

Mantle started only twice in the final 18 games that year and lost the home-run race against Maris 61-54. Against Cincinnati in the World Series, Mantle played in just two games. In a visual that's long been remembered, Mantle got a line-drive base hit and was standing on first base. His hip wound had opened and blood oozed through his uniform and into his stocking.

As gruesome as that story is, McNeer doesn't believe Mantle's death came compliments of Jacobson.

"I can tell you it (hepatitis C) would not have been around for 30 or 35 years inside his body," McNeer said. "The kind of hepatitis he had, he could not have had it that long because it's so progressive. There's no telling how he contracted it, but it was probably in the previous 6-30 months."

After receiving the profile, Mantle stayed in touch with McNeer, but for the wrong reasons.

"We'd talk on the phone every two or three months," McNeer said. "Not about his health, but about golf. I don't think Mickey had a primary doctor. He had a lot of doctors he played golf with."

Because of the family history, Mantle never believed he would live past 40.

"That was something he always wondered about, why he did better than anyone in his family," McNeer said. "It (contracting Hodgkin's disease) is just like having brown eyes or blue eyes. Something from a previous generation doesn't guarantee you'll get one or the other. That (Hodgkin's) was a fear of his. I mean, it was real. It wasn't made up. I think that reinforced his desire to stay off alcohol."

But this wasn't Hodgkin's. This was something else. And this was not something Mantle could conquer by eating right and staying sober.

"Mickey had that letter (the lab profile). He had the doctor recommendations," McNeer said. "But I always wonder what would have happened had he gone to one of those guys on that list. He would tell me, 'Hey, I'm feeling fine.' He was the type person who controlled his

"It left a hole so big that you could put a golf ball in it. P.S. The Yankee front office was furious

own destiny. He knew what he wanted to do and where he wanted to be. He was a person who knew his own mind. I think he thought if he kept off alcohol he'd be OK, or at least be better off."

Smith agreed. "Oh, yeah. I think Mickey thought that; you bet."

Because Mantle was a new patient, McNeer was uncertain which bedside manner to use.

"I'm not a doctor who will sit here and say, 'You're dumb if you don't get this done,' " McNeer said. "No doctor has all the answers. God knows those answers, but I don't. There are no absolutes. I didn't know for sure. I told him there was a high risk of getting liver cancer if the hepatitis C went untreated."

McNeer used another avenue to try to reach Mantle's psyche -- Marshall Smith.

"I talked at length with Marshall," McNeer said. "He was his best friend, or at least one of them. They were just like brothers. They poked and prodded each other throughout the entire exam. If you read what they said in print, it would sound horrible. But it wasn't. Marshall loved Mickey for who he was, a friend. He thought Mickey was a great guy, even without all those home runs."

"I just sort of let him know he had some serious problems with his liver," Smith said. "You couldn't force anything on Mickey. You couldn't say, 'Damn it, I think you should have a liver transplant.' You just couldn't do that with him. I said, 'You need to watch it and maybe think about getting a liver transplant.' I told him just like that. But he sort of evaded it."

McNeer said, "In Mickey's case, he had a lot of pride. If somebody was mean or condescending to him, he just got up and walked. He was one of the easiest people to deal with, as long as you were straight with him and treated him as an equal. He was one of those guys who, what you see is what you get."

In late October, roughly one month after the lab profile initially arrived, Mantle became ill during his Fantasy Baseball camp. Smith contacted McNeer, who faxed copies of Mantle's profile to his Dream Team of hepatitis C specialists. Again, Mantle chose not to contact anyone.

In mid-April of 1995, Mantle became ill at Ben Crenshaw's benefit golf tournament in Austin, Texas. Rather than play golf, Mantle volunteered to sign autographs.

In May, a gravely ill Mantle visited Smith.

"Mickey kept telling me, 'I don't have any strength,' " Smith explained. "He looked awful. His stomach was bloated and he looked yellow (with jaundice)."

On May 27, the Saturday before Memorial Day, Mantle was in Dallas and sought out Smith via telephone at Shangri-La.

"They had been treating him for a hernia at the time," Smith said.

Smith: "Mickey, I think it's your liver."

Mantle: "No, I still think it's a hernia. That's what the doctors think, too."

"The doctors (in Tulsa) wanted me to tell Mickey the truth," Smith said. "Of course, it brought tears to my eyes. Anyway, we contacted a doctor about being admitted and the doctor said he'd be out of town for Memorial Day weekend. I told Mickey, 'They've got to put you in the hospital right now. This is a bunch of bullshit.' He's laying in bed and can't get out of his own house, really."

Mantle wanted to go to the Warren Clinic, which is adjacent to Saint Francis Hospital. "He said, 'I've got to come up there (Tulsa) on Sunday and be admitted,' " Smith said. "Then he said something that tore me up. He said, 'No one's looking after me here.' Nobody seemed to give a damn about him at that time, for whatever reason. Why would he call me in Oklahoma if they had been taking care of him down there?"

The day before Memorial Day, Mantle again telephoned Smith.

Mantle: "Mott, I'm sick."

Smith: "Call an ambulance."

Mantle was so sick, he could not be trans-

Mickey at a news conference in Dallas, Texas; July 1995.

ported to his desired location in Tulsa. Instead, Mantle was taken to the Baylor University Medical Center in Dallas. "When he got there, all his records were sent from Tulsa," Smith said. "Everything they had found at the Warren Clinic was what they had found down there."

"We were going to bring him up here on Memorial Day," McNeer said. "But I knew what was going on just from the symptoms he was describing over the phone. So I recommended him to doctors in Dallas."

Mantle: "I want to get my liver there."

McNeer: "We don't do liver transplants here, Mickey."

Mantle: "You do those heart transplants, right?"

McNeer: "Yeah, that's true. But that's a totally different thing."

Mantle had formed a solid relationship with McNeer.

"He's a great guy," Smith said of McNeer. "It was obvious he loved Mickey. He kept up with Mickey the whole time. He tried, probably harder than anybody, to get Mickey the kind of help he needed for (liver) rehabilitation."

"Mickey once said, 'There are some doctors who are great at talking to 1,500 people at a medical seminar, and there are doctors who take care of patients,' " McNeer said. "I was complimented that he wanted to come up here. As sick as he sounded on the phone, I knew he had to stay in Dallas."

It wasn't until June 5 that it was publicly announced Mantle would require a liver transplant. On June 8, he underwent a 7 1/2-hour operation.

Smith first saw Mantle five days later. "He had all these IVs in him and that kind of stuff," Smith said.

Mantle (whispering): "Hey, Mott."

Smith: "Hey, Mick. How you feelin'?"

Mantle: "How in the hell do you think I'm feelin'?"

Smith: "Now we know who's the healthiest, huh? You owe me $100."

Mantle: "Get outta here. I'm gonna make it."

Female workers at Shangri-La had gotten Mantle a bath robe. Inside one pocket were a bunch of cards sending him best wishes. In the other pocket was a fake snake, Mantle's favorite prop for any occasion.

"I didn't want to pull out that snake. I was afraid he'd throw up a liver," Smith said jokingly.

Unable to fight the urge, Smith pulled out the snake and flashed it at Mantle.

Nurse: "Why are you doing that?"

Mantle: "Oh, he's just playing a joke we used play. But I don't feel like a joke right now."

> **"I** *didn't want to pull out that snake. I was afraid he'd throw up a liver"*

A tear ran down Mantle's cheek as he spoke.

Within three weeks, Mantle was back in his Dallas home. When he felt better, Mantle planned to visit Smith at Shangri-La. In the meantime, he occasionally rode in a golf cart at his "home away from home", Preston Trail Golf Club, putting up bets for his kids to play against one another. Mantle tried to work out by walking on a treadmill.

"He telephoned every morning between 7:30 and 8:30," Smith said. "What the hell we talked about, I have no idea. He had checkups all the time at the (Baylor) hospital and was on a lot of medication."

One day in late July, reports began to circulate that Mantle wasn't as healthy as everybody believed. Smith, as he often does, got defensive about Mantle. "I really got upset," Smith said. "Of course, I'm a positive person and I didn't want to believe it. Around 7 or 8 that night, I heard they had found cancer."

Three days before Mantle's death, Smith went to the hospital to see Mickey, who was sitting in a chair watching a golf tournament. Among those to visit that day were former teammates Whitey Ford, Bill "Moose" Skowron, Bobby Richardson, Hank Bauer, Johnny Blanchard and several members of the Mantle family.

"He was weak," Smith described. "All that muscle of his had turned to flab. It was just hanging from his body. Gosh, I wish I hadn't seen him that way. Little Mickey asked me to come in about 5 or 6 the next morning so he could go and visit his baby girl at home. Of course, it was my pleasure."

Although barely coherent, Mantle's wit was intact.

Around 7 a.m., a nurse came into the room and wanted to change Mantle's pajamas, which were drenched in sweat.

Nurse: "Mr. Mantle, I have to take off your pajamas."

Mantle: "What, and have a little fun?"

A little while later, Mantle asked Smith to help him to the urinal. "Although I don't think you or I are strong enough to get me to the bathroom," Mantle said.

Incredibly frail, Mantle awkwardly asked Smith for a little "help."

Smith: "Have you been circumcised?"

Mantle: "No, have you?"

"I stood near him in the bathroom to make sure he didn't fall," Smith said. "Mickey said, 'You're bothering the hell out of me. I can't go if you're looking at me.' I backed off and he went to bathroom. Then he said, 'Help me get over there so I can look out the window.' "

> **"If you have any business to talk to Mickey about, you need to talk to him now."**

Smith pulled up the shades and Mantle stared out the window for several minutes.

Smith: "What the devil are you looking at?"

Mantle: "I'm just looking at all the green grass, that road over there and all those cars going by."

Smith began to cry.

Around 10:30 a.m. with Mantle asleep, a doctor came into the room with Mantle's lawyer, Roy True. "If you have any business to talk to Mickey about, you need to talk to him now," the doctor told True.

Almost on cue, Mantle awakened.

Smith: "Mick, I'm gonna go. I'll see you a little bit later."

Mantle: "Please don't go."

Smith: "Roy needs to talk to you about some things."

Mantle: "Aw, he bugs the hell out of me. Please don't go."

Smith: "I'll be back."

Mantle: "If you don't come back, will you call?"

Smith: "Sure, Mick. I'll call."

Smith never spoke to his best friend again.

Early Sunday morning, on Aug. 13, 1995, with wife Merlyn and son David by his side, Mickey Charles Mantle died of cancer at age 63.

Meeting the Mick

Marshall McLemore Smith was born on June 10, 1926, in far northeast Oklahoma. The town name is Quapaw, pronounced QWA-paw.

Roughly 8 miles to the southwest is Miami, pronounced my-AM-uh.

Roughly 4 miles to the west is Commerce, no pronunciation guide necessary.

It is in these three towns where Smith has lived and worked most of his life. He was born there, raised there, left there, visited there, relocated there, still lives there, and likely will die there. Consider this his love triangle.

After the first 70 years of his life, Smith could be found 8 miles from his birthplace. He resides in Miami, a smooth 7-iron away from Miami Golf & Country Club and a 30-minute drive from the Shangri-La Resort on Grand Lake. Smith, a former club pro who began taking golf lessons at age 5, wouldn't have it any other way.

Commerce is best known as the town which

Mickey playing for the Yankees Joplin, Missouri Class C farm team in 1949.

Mutt Mantle with his son, Mickey, in '33.

produced Mickey Mantle, which isn't exactly accurate. Mantle actually was born roughly 40 miles to the south in Spavinaw. He moved to Commerce at age 4. It was there his life took direction. From sandlot teams, to the Whiz Kids, to the Independence (Kan.) Yankees, to the Joplin (Mo.) Miners, to the New York Yankees, to baseball's Hall of Fame.

"Spavinaw is an Indian name," Mantle once wrote. "As a small boy living in Commerce, I heard many stories about the Cherokees, the Chickasaws, the Creeks, and the other Oklahoma tribes, stories told mostly by my dad's friends who remembered driving their wagons over muddy roads past sorry-looking Indian cabins and afterward pulling into town, hitching their horses and watering them at troughs smelling of sulfur."

Miami is best known as the town which produced 1969 Heisman Trophy winner Steve Owens, which isn't exactly accurate. Owens actually was born roughly 110 miles to the south in Gore. He moved to Miami at age 6. It was there where his life took direction. His football career progressed from the Miami Wardogs, to the Oklahoma Sooners, to the Detroit Lions.

"It was good for me to move to Miami because back then Gore didn't even have a football team," Owens said. "If I hadn't left Gore -- who knows? -- I might never have even seen a football. It's hard to imagine what the hell I would have done with myself if that had happened."

Quapaw is best known as the town which produced, uh ... Who? Or what? "Quapaw looks best covered in snow," Smith began. "It has the only Christmas parade in the world where the parade stands still and people walk around. And it's only 1,540 miles southwest of New York City." During its heyday, Quapaw was in one of the world's largest zinc and lead mining districts.

Not coincidentally, Smith, Mantle and Owens eventually grew to be as close as their towns. This was their friendship triangle.

Smith knew Mantle from the fall of 1947 up to Mantle's death in August of 1995. By that time, Owens' friendship with Mantle was in its third decade. When Mantle was around, he constantly "needled" Smith. With Mantle now gone, Owens took control.

"If you talk to Marshall long enough, you'll think he taught Mantle everything he did -- how to golf, how to bat, how to throw," Owens said, smiling at Smith. "Nah, I'm just kiddin' ya, Marshall."

"Mick's gone and I still put up with this crap," Smith said, shaking his head. "Aw, I love it."

Smith and Mantle met on a high school football field. The Commerce Tigers vs. the Quapaw Wildcats. Rival members of the Lucky Seven Conference.

Mantle claimed the score was "something like 47-0." Smith insists the final was 6-0. Either way, Commerce was victorious, as it often was in those days.

Mickey in '49.

Mickey at age 15

Steve Owens, Marshall Smith and Mickey. Shangri-la; Winter '72.

Commerce H.S. football field.

Having returned from a 2 1/2-year stint in the Navy prior to his senior year, Smith was more mature and had better instincts than many of his teammates. That age difference came in handy for outsmarting opponents and having a keen sense of where the play was headed. When that didn't work, superior athleticism took over.

This came in the form of Mickey Mantle.

"Mickey would have been the greatest football player, boxer, anything," Smith said. "He had so much talent. Mickey was like a cat. Both of us were quick, but he was 10 times as quick as me. Mickey could run like a deer. You'd have to tackle him at the line of scrimmage because nobody could catch Mickey once he got in the open."

Smith and Mantle were teammates on a basketball team for most of one season. Both played guard. Smith said he was more of a scorer. Mantle, meanwhile, was more of everything else.

""He and I called it semi-pro, but it was really just an independent basketball league," Smith said. "We played before packed houses at places all over the tri-state area. I'll tell you what, we were a pretty doggone good team, too. When we won, we got steaks. If we lost, we got hamburgers.

Pump house in Cardin, Oaklahoma.

"I remember playing at the YMCA in Joplin one time against this really good team. (Pro football Hall-of-Famer) Jim Finks and all those football players would try to drive Mick and us into the walls. Pretty soon, Mickey had to quit. The Yankees found out he was playing. They eventually came down and made him stop. They were afraid he'd get hurt.

"You talk about guys getting five or six steals (in one basketball game), Mickey was liable to get 10-12 steals. I'm serious," Smith said, his voice cracking. "He was a real good defensive player and a real good rebounder, but a poor shot. Nobody had the reflexes Mickey had. Nobody had the speed he had."

That speed came from when Mantle lived in Whitebird. He would take a school bus to an old pump house in Cardin, which was one mile away from his home (along a gravel road). Mantle wasn't

Commerce H.S. varsity basketball team; '47.

particularly fond of the dark.

"He was so scared, he'd run as fast as he could because he was afraid somebody was going to grab him," Smith said.

"Blackbirds would fly up alongside the road, their wings flapping like mad, and I'd visualize all these ghost stories that came from the miners," Mantle wrote. "Weird tales about murders, people being thrown into caved-in holes around the mills; a perfect spot if you wanted to commit a crime and bury the evidence without ever getting caught. Come to think of it, I didn't know of any actual murders. Why would anyone be killed in the first place? You couldn't rob anybody. Nobody had anything ... I was scared to death of the dark. I must have run that mile in less than four minutes -- long before Roger Bannister thought of it. I didn't even feel my feet touch the ground until I reached home."

Mantle's reflexes and quickness were aided by chasing rabbits in open fields. "Nobody told him to do it," Smith said. "It was no scheme. He just didn't know any better."

This from a kid who battled a severe case of osteomyelitis (staph infection of the bone marrow) as a teenager after being kicked in the left shin during football practice. By the next day, Mantle had a fever of 104 and his ankle had swollen to twice its normal size. The injury was slow to heal and one doctor suggested amputating the leg. Mantle's mother said, "The hell you are."

Mickey and Yankee Hall of Famer Casey Stengel in '51.

Soon, Mantle would be transferred to the Crippled Children's Hospital in Oklahoma City, some 190 miles away. In the end, Mantle's leg was saved by a miracle drug named penicillin.

From osteomyelitis to the four-minute mile. A regular Forrest Gump.

"I don't think he ever talked to anybody about this but me," Smith said, "but one time he said, 'Whether they're white or black, I don't think there's anybody out there who could outrun me.' Time and time again people wanted to bet they could outrun him, but no one ever plunked the

JR. CARDINAL LEAGUE WINNERS 1948 "CHAMPION'S
WON 40 LOST 17

TOP: Baxter Springs, Kansas Junior Cardinal League "Whiz Kids" baseball team, 48 League Champions.

BOTTOM: Baxter Springs, Kansas "Whiz Kids" baseball team, '47 League Champions.

money down. Everybody chickened out."

"The fastest slugger I ever saw," Yankees manager Casey Stengel often said of Mantle.

"If I could run like that son of a bitch, I'd hit .400 every year," said Red Sox Hall of Famer Ted Williams, the last man to break the magical barrier (1941).

And yet Mickey would steal only 153 bases in an 18-year career, his most prolific season coming in 1959 with 21.

There were two big reasons for this: 1) The powerful Yankees were hardly a station-to-station ballclub. They preferred trotting around the bases rather than stealing them. Mantle had a career slugging percentage of .557 and did show his speed with 72 career triples; 2) From his rookie season on, Mantle constantly battled leg injuries.

It was said that Mantle ran to first in 3.1 seconds from the first-base side of the plate and 3.5 seconds from the third-base side, clockings that would challenge today's best.

As superb an athlete as Mantle was, he wasn't

Mickey and Merlyn Mantle on their wedding day in '51.

Head stone for Mickey's parents Mutt and Lovell Mantle.

the class stud in athletics. That distinction belonged to one of his closest friends at the time, basketball and football star Bill Mosely.

The University of Oklahoma recruited Mantle to play football. (Smith said Mosely actually was the one the Sooners wanted, and Mantle more or less stumbled into becoming a recruit simply by hanging around.)

"There was this time in 1949 when I was a senior in Commerce High School and they brought me down to OU to work out," Mantle said in a lengthy interview with television commentator Bob Costas. "I never did meet (head coach) Bud Wilkinson, but (quarterback) Darrell Royal drove me all around the campus, I knew who he was, but he never could remember my name. He probably didn't even think about it, but in 1958 I was living in Dallas, Texas, and the Texas Longhorns were playing at Fort Worth, against TCU. I went to the game and they gave me a pass to go down on the field. It was right after the World Series and I met

Billy Martin with Mickey and his twin brothers Ray and Roy Mantle.

Darrell Royal (head coach for Texas) and he goes, 'Hey, nice meeting you. I always wanted to meet you.' I said, 'Darrell, I met you a long time ago. Don't you remember?' I said, 'You drove me around Oklahoma University in your car one day and showed me all the dormitories and tried to talk me into coming to OU to play football.' He said, 'In 1949?' I said, 'Yeah.' He said, 'Hell, you weren't even Mickey Mantle then.' ''

Smith laughed as he retold the story. "Mick just never realized he was Mickey Mantle," Smith said.

Mosely would go on to play football at Pittsburg State Teachers College in Kansas. Mantle would go to Yankee Stadium in New York City.

Mickey's father was Elven Clark "Mutt" Mantle. The precise spelling of his first name is somewhat of a mystery.

A) Mickey spelled his father's name Elvin and named his first son Mickey Elvin.

B) On Mutt Mantle's driver's license, his first name was spelled Elvan.

C) His headstone reads Elven, as it does on the birth certificate of his youngest son, Larry (Butch).

Because it was Mutt's wife, Lovell, who ordered the inscription on the headstone, it is believed C is the proper spelling.

"I'm not sure how he spelled his name," said

Billy Martin with Mickey and Mickey, Jr.

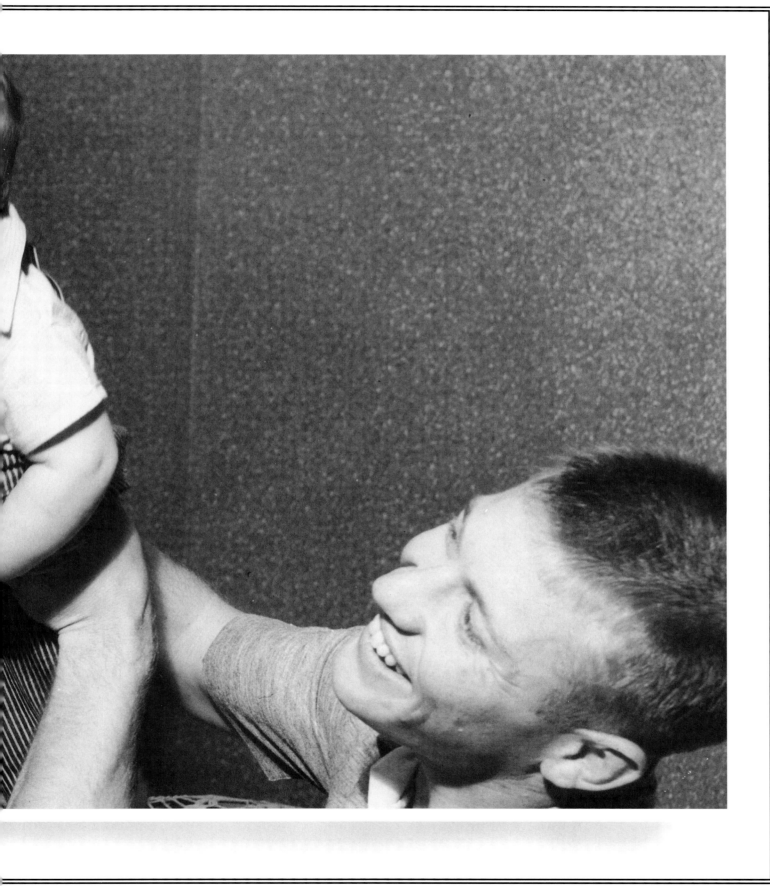

Merlyn and Mickey with their children: Danny, Billy, David, and Mickey, Jr. in '59.

Merlyn and Mickey with the boys in '60.

Mickey giving his son Danny putting tips; Dallas Texas, '61.

Barbara, the Mutt and Lovell's lone daughter. "The only way I ever saw him sign anything was 'E.C. Mantle.' "

Elven died in 1952 at age 40. Lovell died in 1995, just five months before Mickey, at age 91. Mickey's parents were layed to rest side-by-side at GAR (Grand Army of the Republic) Cemetery between Miami and Commerce. Sadly, more than 18 months after Lovell's passing, the year of her death had yet to be inscribed on the headstone.

Mickey was the eldest of the Mantle children, followed by twins Ray and Roy, Barbara and Larry. There also was half brother Theodore and half sister Anna, who died young and was not raised by the family.

Mickey was born in a two-room, unpainted hilltop house on the north edge of Spavinaw. There were no streets, only a narrow dirt road through the corn and wheat fields.

When the Mantles moved to Commerce, their first residence was at 319 South Quincy Street. There, Mickey began to learn how to switch-hit at age 6.

Mutt had named his first son after Gordon Stanley "Mickey" Cochran, a Hall of Fame catcher with the Philadelphia Athletics and Detroit Tigers and a lifetime .320 hitter. The year Mickey Mantle was born, Mickey Cochran hit .349. Cochran's namesake would more than quadruple his lifetime home run total of 119.

Mutt Mantle would constantly play catch with

Mickey with Josephine H. Smith (Marshall's Mom)

his son. There also was batting practice, and plenty of it. When his right-handed father threw, Mickey batted from the left side. When his left-handed grandfather Charlie threw, Mickey took swings from the right side. At first, it was lollygag stuff with tennis balls. In time, their two-hour hitting sessions routinely include a fare share of brush-backs.

"No boy, I think, ever loved his father more than I did," Mantle said shortly before he retired prior to the 1969 season. "I was a good boy, really, who needed little disciplining, and I would do nearly anything to keep my father happy. He was a big, strong, stern-looking man, just a fraction short of 6 feet tall, lean and well-muscled, with the strong, gnarled hands of a miner, and dark, thick hair ... He never had to raise his hand to me to make me obey. I needed only a sharp look or a word from him and the

Mickey and Marshall Smith at Barton Creek Resort in Austin, Texas; April '95.

knowledge that I had displeased him made me go and do better."

Mickey indeed did better than any switch-hitter in the history of the game in terms of power.

While Pete Rose swatted singles, Mantle banged balls off the outfield bleachers.

From Commerce, the Mantle family moved to a nearby farm in the country. There was no plumbing and plenty of chores to do. Lovell despised the place.

From there, they moved to Dr. Wormington's farm, where there were still more chores, and no plumbing. Again, Lovell despised the place.

From there, they moved back to Commerce into a nice seven-bedroom house Mickey purchased after his rookie season with the Yankees in 1951. "Plenty of space for the family," Mantle said of the 317 South River address. "We also had our own phone. Two rings meant us."

Shortly after his father's death, Mickey and wife, Merlyn, built a $16,000 house at 319 South Maple Street across town from his mother's house.

Roughly five years later, Mickey, Merlyn, Mickey Jr., David and Billy (Danny was yet to be born), packed up and moved to 5730 Watson Circle in Dallas. Reasons for their departure will be dis-

Mickey and Billy Martin outside the Hotel Edison in New York City. Note the date, 12/25/89, the day after Billy Martin died.

cussed later.

In the end, Mickey and Danny would reside in a condo near Preston Trail Golf Club.

Mantle's favorite holiday wasn't even an official holiday -- April Fools' Day.

"He'd call you and tell you your house was on fire or somethin'," Smith said.

Mantle got so out of hand, he literally became a snake in the grass. His favorite prank.

"He'd scout out play snakes everywhere," Smith said, shaking his head. "Copperheads, water moccasin, all kinds. He'd leave a snake coiled up for a maid in the hotel room. Once, at my office, he hid a snake inside the desk drawer. It scared our daughters to death."

Mantle's least favorite holiday was Christmas. Without question. Every year. Second to none.

"He was always sad," Smith explained. "He always put on the biggest drunk at Christmas time, and stayed that way."

Why?

"I think it was because he missed his father," said Smith's wife, Corinne.

When Mantle went to the Betty Ford Center in

early 1994 to treat his alcohol abuse, he was instructed to write a letter to his father. Mantle later said he cried through the 10 minutes it took him to write the letter.

"He wouldn't tell me what it said because he said it would have embarrassed him," Smith recalled. "I asked him if he still had the letter. He said he took it out and burned it. He didn't want anybody to see what he wrote."

Late in his life, Mantle became closer and closer to his mother, who was in a nursing home at nearby Jay, Okla. Half brother Theodore also was close to his mother. He and Mantle often visited together, alongside Marshall and Corinne Smith.

"It was so warm to watch him with his mama," Smith said. "Every time he'd leave, he'd seem so sad. He thought it was too bad she was still living because of her state of mind (with Alzheimer's disease).

"He would always talk about that death doctor, Dr. Jack Kevorkian, who assists terminally ill patients with suicide," Smith said. "Mickey always thought that was right, the right thing to do. He couldn't stand to see his mother like that. She'd remember me as 'the golfer,' but half the time she didn't remember him. When you're that sick and you don't remember things, that's sad to see. But when she did recognize Mickey, she'd perk up."

Mantle thought his mother would outlive him, and she nearly did. Lovell Mantle died on March 19, 1995. Mickey Mantle died on Aug. 13, 1995.

"Mickey truthfully never thought he would lived to be 40," Smith said.

Why would he, given his family history of Hodgkin's disease afflicting the Mantle men?

"Talk about being poor, and not having anything," Smith said. "That's what it was like living in the heart of the lead and zinc mines. You can talk about Harlem and any other place in the country, but around here, you couldn't escape it. ''

Smith admits he got a bit too sensitive about Mickey, who often was referred to as a "country bumpkin." The term carries a double-meaning. That person is either incredibly stupid, or his naivete makes him incredibly lovable.

To Smith, it was always the latter, never the first.

"Oh, I was defensive all the time," Smith said. "I probably got into more (verbal) fights, over that issue, than he ever did. Mickey had a good mind. He was no dummy."

When Mantle was a senior at Commerce High School, there was an English composition contest at Northeastern Oklahoma A&M, a junior college in Miami.

"Mickey had the highest score," Smith said. "That was one of the highlights of his life, but nobody knows that story. He never let me forget it,

Late in his life, Mantle became closer and closer to his mother, who lived in a nursing home at nearby Jay, Okla.

though. He'd say, 'You never won anything like that.' He always reminded me how much smarter he was than me, and he probably was. He could breeze through crossword puzzles."

Mantle was no country bumpkin, Smith insisted. "He was just a "Good ole Boy."

And polite ... at least when he was sober.

"Mickey had so much charisma," Smith said. "He was a sharp dresser. He watched his English. He watched his manners at the table. Mickey learned a lot for someone coming from such a little place in Oklahoma. He learned manners from watching other people, and that's how he taught other people. Merlyn once went out and bought a book on etiquette. All those things are why Mickey was always insecure about himself."

"When he went into the Yankees' locker room, he didn't think you were supposed to wear your baseball shoes, so he took them off. He didn't know bell boys were supposed to carry your bags. I was the first one to tell him that, in Kansas City. He learned the social end about how to dress and so forth. He was like the All-American boy. When he got dressed up and put on a suit, no matter what he put on, he looked great."

One more thing. "Nobody ever picked up the tab quicker than Mickey Mantle," Smith said. "He wasn't a fumbler when it came to buying things for people. Mick always carried way too much money on him, often several thousand dollars. He preferred cash to credit cards or checks. He never wanted a scandal to his name, so he was very careful about paying his taxes."

Smith said he and Mantle were closest in the last four or five years of Mantle's life.

"As I think back to all the time we spent together, wherever I was, he'd come to me," Smith said. "Whether it was in Independence, or New Mexico, or the Bahamas. Wherever it was, he made it a point to come see me. I never realized all that until after he died. You talk about Mickey not realizing things, I just didn't realize what a true friend he was.

"I couldn't brag on him if he was here with me. But since he's not with us, I can say he was a little extra special."

And there were times, particularly in those final years, when Mantle said the same of Smith. Not to his face, of course. It didn't work that way. Smith was forced to find out second-hand.

"Mickey was always pulling for the underdog," Smith said. "He probably looked at me as an underdog, so he always treated me nice."

> **W**hen he went into the Yankees' locker room he didn't think you were supposed to wear your baseball shoes, so he took them off

TEE TIME

It was after the 1955 season and Mickey Mantle wanted to play golf with some of his New York Yankees teammates. "Come back when you're good enough," Yogi Berra told him.

At the time, Mantle and the Yankees were playing 24 exhibition games in the Far East. Mantle made up a phony excuse that he had to return to Commerce because his wife, Merlyn, was expecting their second child at any moment. Two months later, on Dec. 26, David was born. Yankees general manager George Weiss informed baseball commissioner Ford Frick that Mantle had failed to fulfill his exhibition commitment. Frick promptly fined Mantle. "The only thing that made me sore was that Weiss didn't even have the courtesy to congratulate Merlyn," Mantle once said.

It was during this time Mantle sought the tutelage of Marshall Smith, then a club pro at Independence (Kan.) Country Club. Mantle had

Mickey taking a break during a '89 Penthouse Magazine interview.

taken up the game a couple of years earlier, but not seriously.

"Mickey had been playing left-handed the first two years," Smith recalled. "The first thing I did was make him switch to right-handed. Wilson (Sporting Goods) wanted to give him a free set of right-handed clubs, and Mickey was amazed they wanted to do something like that for him. (Cost for the clubs, bag and head covers -- $322.50, no strings attached.)

"He could really drive the ball, although he sometimes had his troubles around the greens. Most baseball players can hit the ball real well. They know how to turn their bodies without swaying to get the full power into their swing. The pivot at the hips is similar in golf and baseball."

Why the switch to the right side? "Normally, most of the golf courses are laid out for right-handers," Smith explained. "It was easier to work with him and get him to swing right-handed than left-handed. His worst habit was coming over the top of the ball. He was swinging outside-in rather than

Mickey in a custom built golf cart alongside the signature tent during his golf tournament at Shangri-La, Okla.

Mickey checking out a peculiar looking putter with Witey Ford and Joe DiMaggio in '78.

Mickey, Whitey and Joe "D" at the same '78 golf tournament.

Mickey is unhappy as he misses a put in the National Baseball Players' Golf Tournament at Miami, Florida in February '67.

Mickey's powerful golf swing in the late fall at Shangri-La.

Mickey hitting from a poor lie with a gallery in attendance.

inside-out. He had a big ol' slice (left-to-right spin on the ball). We cured it real quick. We just kept his right elbow in, pointing it down to the ground. He stayed behind the ball and used his fingers and hands more. He stayed behind the ball probably better than any golfer, including anybody on tour, that I've ever seen."

The most powerful switch-hitter in baseball history started out as a 20-25 handicap. Within a few years under Smith's guidance, he was down to a 3 or 4. "But he'd always tell people he was about a 10 or 12 because he'd always be betting," Smith said with a chuckle. "Nobody could drive the golf ball like him. He had so much clubhead speed and hand action. Great balance, too. He'd set back on his right side, just like in baseball, which gets you another 8-10 inches on the pitcher. He'd call me about baseball all the time when he got to swaying back and forth while hitting and striking out. He would relate that to golf and I think it helped him out a bit."

Smith is a long believer in the K.I.S.S. method to golf -- Keep It Simple, Stupid.

He learned it from the late Ky Laffoon, a standout tour professional in the 1930s and '40s who often helped out Ben Hogan:

Draw the club back. Then release it.

End of lesson.

"Your two thumbs look up at God at the top of your backswing and again at the top of your finish," explained Smith, who still gives lessons at

Mickey and Marshall at Shangri-La.

Shangri-La Resort in Afton, Okla., in Joplin, Mo., and at various other places. "Forget your upper body. Forget your lower body. They just go along for the ride, passive-like. It's all in the arms. You start turning them over as soon as you can and keep turning them."

Mantle and Smith often paired up during competitions (remember Mantle's alleged handicap?). "We'd play all winter, seemed like every day," Smith said. "It didn't matter what the temperature was. Even if it was 18 above zero, we'd golf. No question about it. Mickey just loved that game."

"Once upon a time" they were both young.

Mickey always focused on staying behind the ball.

During their rounds together, Mantle and Smith would make plans. "We'd talk about what we're going to do with the money we were about to win," Smith said. "We'd compare it to going to the ballpark. First, we'd get into the park by winning the first couple holes. Then we'd buy some popcorn, then a drink, then some memorabilities. We didn't talk about losing, and we didn't lose very often, either."

The average stakes were $500-$1,000 per round. "But sometimes there were carryovers worth $3,000-$5,000," Smith said. The format was always team best ball.

Mantle abhored losing. "I never saw anybody who hated to lose more than Mickey did," Smith said. "He was a competitive SOB. But he never got mad at the people he was playing against, only himself."

Mantle often showed his anger while playing baseball. At the outset of his professional career in the minor leagues, he often would take out his frustrations on unsuspecting water coolers --

1	2	3	4	5	6	7	8	9	OUT	9-HOLE NOTES
440	423	401	535	186	385	536	192	438	3536	3-9-82
423	407	383	511	171	363	513	172	424	3367	
407	389	369	477	156	338	488	152	410	3186	
4	4	4	5	3	4	5	3	4	36	
6	5	6	6	4	4	8	3	5	45	
5	5	6	5	4	4	5	4	5		
3	9	11	5	15	13	1	17	7		
4	5	5	5	4	4	5	3	4		
5	5	5	5	3	4	5	4	5		
393	373	354	449	133	320	434	137	389	2982	
4	4	4	5	3	4	5	3	5	37	

CORAL RIDGE COUNTRY CLUB
FORT LAUDERDALE, FLORIDA

Score card from the Coral Ridge C.C., Ft. Lauderdale, Florida. Golf match between Mickey and Whitey Ford vs. Marshall and "Little" Marshall Smith.

	10	11	12	13	14	15	16	17	18	IN	OUT	TOT 18	HDCP	NET
CHAMPIONSHIP COURSE	434	541	194	572	439	353	184	397	423	3537	3536	7073		
LONG COURSE	421	514	179	558	423	334	169	383	403	3384	3367	6751		
REGULAR COURSE	406	492	164	526	400	317	154	362	389	3210	3186	6396		
PAR	4	5	3	5	4	4	3	4	4	36	36	72		
+ — 0														
Mott	5	6	3	6	6	5		4	5	44	45	89		
Marshall	5	4	4	6		5	4	4				89		
HANDICAP STROKES	10	④	18	②	⑥	14	16	12	8					
Mick	5	5	4	5	4	5	3	4				81		
Ford	6	5	4	6	8	4	4	5	7			89		
LADIES COURSE	386	469	149	485	378	300	139	345	373	3024	2982	6006		
PAR	4	5	3	5	4	4	3	4	5	37	37	74		
+ — 0														

Coral Ridge Country Club (89)
FORT LAUDERDALE, FLORIDA
Course Designed By - Robert Trent Jones   Golf Professional - Lew Worsham
United States Golf Association Rules Govern Play

nice going Ford

LOCAL RULES
Out of bounds defined by white stakes
Water Hazards — Yellow lines and stakes
Lateral Water Hazards — Red line and stakes
Ball may be dropped from all blacktopped pathways and roads at nearest point of relief no nearer to hole without penalty.
Please observe cart traffic ropes and signs. Please smooth out footprints when leaving sand traps and repair ball marks made on greens. Slow players must yield right of way.
Yardage markers indicate distance to center of green:
Red - 100 yds.   White - 150 yds.   Blue - 200 yds.

Player_____

Score Attested by _____

Date _____

Championship — Blue ★ Long — White ★ Regular — Red ★ Ladies — Yellow
Course Rating — 72.9   71.3   69.9   73.2

spilling them, kicking them, hitting them, throwing them. He quickly became known as "King of the Broken Water Coolers" and continued this particular ritual in the major leagues.

Throughout his career, Mantle also pounded more than one fist into a wall, screamed more than one obscenity and displayed more than one obscene gesture to hecklers in the crowd. One year during spring training in St. Petersburg, Fla., a disgusted Mantle nearly threw his bat completely out of the stadium behind the first-base dugout after hitting an infield pop-up.

His anger also showed in golf. Laffoon was known for his temper. Smith did not pass that trait along to his students, who have included Chi Chi Rodriguez, Gary Player, Craig Stadler, Walt Zembriski, Woody Blackburn, and professional athletes from many other sports, including former NBA player Scott Hastings.

When the Mantle family first moved to Dallas in 1957, Mickey played at Glen Lakes, which has since been replaced with office buildings and an expressway. "We grew closer when he moved to Dallas," Smith said. "We spent more time together there because he always had a big hustling game going."

Mantle was an amateur version of Tommy Bolt. Tempestuous Tommy and Manic Mickey.

"They had a big lake there," Smith recalled of the Glen Lakes course, "and Mickey threw plenty of clubs into that lake. Pretty soon, you could walk across it standing on all the clubs that were in there. Mickey got this solid gold putter (from New York City hobnobber Toots Shor) with a diamond

Mickey's famous snake gag!

on top of the face where you lined up the putt. Mickey missed a putt and sent that thing sailing into the lake. I told him how much it was probably worth and he had all these caddies out there trying to locate it. He never got it back, though. He threw his whole set in there once, golf bag and all. He had to get those back, though. His car keys were in the bag."

With Mantle at the plate, it was all or nothing. In his 18-year career, he had 536 home runs and 1,710 strikeouts. His predecessor Joe DiMaggio, a remarkable study of skill and discipline, had 361 home runs and just 369 strikeouts in his 13-year career.

Mantle was no different, off the tee, in golf. He'd see trouble -- a lake, a creek, a fairway bunker, a row of trees -- and do everything in his power to clear any or all hazards with one swing of the club.

Mantle and Smith often played at Southern Hills Country Club in Tulsa. Tales of Mantle's mighty feats there are legendary.

Mickey and "The Babe" launching homeruns.

Southern Hills Country Club COURSE RATINGS: BLUE 74   WHITE 72   RED 70

HOLE	1	2	3	4	5	6	7	8	9	OUT	10	11	12	13	14	15	16	17	18	IN	TO
BLUE TEES	459	450	410	360	585	177	401	218	378	3438	378	167	465	545	210	410	500	346	420	3441	687
WHITE TEES	459	405	380	340	565	160	379	208	367	3263	375	151	421	529	191	375	482	333	401	3258	652
RED TEES	459	395	358	327	535	151	359	202	359	3146	362	141	406	500	173	358	454	328	392	3114	626
PAR	4	4	4	4	5	3	4	3	4	35	4	3	4	5	3	4	5	4	4	36	7
MANTLE	6	4	4	5	6	5	5	4	4		4	4	5	7	4	5	4	3	4		
Matt	4	4	4	4	5	3	5	4	5		4	4	4	5	3	4	5	5	4		
Mc Phit	4	4	3	4	4	4	5	3	4	35	5	1	4	5	4	4	5	3	4	41	76
Tandy	6	7	5	4	7	4	5	4	4		4	4	6	8	1	4		5	5		
WE											3										
THEY											3	4	3	4							
HANDICAP	11	3	7	15	1	17	13	5	9		12	18	6	2	16	10	4	14	8		

DATE_____   SCORER_____   ATTESTED_____

85% Foursome Match Play Handicap Allowances
1-1	5-4	9-8	13-11	17-14	21-18
2-2	6-5	10-9	14-12	18-15	22-19
3-3	7-6	11-9	15-13	19-16	23-20
4-3	8-7	12-10	16-14	20-17	24-20

INDIVIDUAL — Full difference.

TALLY SHEET

Name		Total

Southern Hills
COUNTRY CLUB
TULSA, OKLA.

MEN'S
SCORE CARD

U. S. G. A. Rules govern with these exceptions:

Paved Roads and Cart Paths are obstructions, lift and drop without penalty.

Mickey (Little Ben) Mantle's score card at Southern Hills C.C. in March of '82.

Mickey and granddaughter in '94.

'95 Private Club caricature of Mickey, Loni Anderson and Yogi Berra.

If you
could play
a round
with
anyone in
the world,
who would
be your
partner?
Some
golfers
share their
fairway
fantasies.

LETTERING BY BERHARD HAISHER

BY DAN GLEASON
ILLUSTRATIONS BY PHILIP BURKE

Mickey Mantle, baseball legend, Greensboro, Georgia
He says his dream golf partners would be "Loni Anderson or
Yogi Berra. That's both ends of the spectrum. Enough said."

Mickey Mantle's

Third Annual Ballplayers Banquet

Feb. 1st & 2nd, 1963

Mickey Mantle

GUEST LIST

Hank Bauer	Baltimore Orioles
Bob Cerv	New York Mets
Eddie Fisher	Chicago White Sox
Gene Green	Cleveland Indians
Tom Greenwade	New York Yankees
Whitey Herzog	Detroit Tigers
Ron Hunt	New York Mets
Rod Kanehl	New York Mets
Don Lock	Washington Senators
Sherm Lollar	Chicago White Sox
Jerry Lumpe	Kansas City Athletics
Mickey Mantle	New York Yankees
Roger Maris	New York Yankees
Cal McLish	Philadelphia Phillies
Del Rice	Los Angeles Angels
John Sain	New York Yankees
Norm Siebern	Kansas City Athletics
Tom Sturdivant	Pittsburgh Pirates
Lee Thomas	Los Angeles Angels
Bill Tuttle	Minnesota Twins
Bill Virdon	Pittsburgh Pirates
Jack White	New York Yankees
H. D. Youngman	New York Yankee Auxiliary

And all their lovely wives.

FRIDAY, FEBRUARY 1, 1963

Check into your room and come on over to Room 124.

2:30 PM to 5:30 PM ... BOWLING
for men and women at Plaza Lanes. Arrangements have been made for lanes, balls, shoes and refreshments. Just order what you want from the lounge and from the snack bar; Mickey will pick up the tab. Prizes will be awarded for the best 3-line total for men and for women.

... GOLF
for men at Twin Hills Golf and Country Club, weather permitting.

... RELAX
if you don't want to golf or bowl, just plain loafing is possible in Room 124 or in the Cocktail Lounge at the motel.

5:30 PM to 7:00 PM ... NOTHING PLANNED
you're on your own.

7:00 PM to 8:00 PM ... COCKTAIL PARTY
in The Dugout.

8:00 PM to 9:30 PM ... BUFFET DINNER
in The Red Carpet Room.

9:00 PM to 9:45 PM ... FLOOR SHOW
Somethin' Smith & The Redheads' first show.

9:45 PM to 10:30 PM ... DANCING
The Toby Oster Trio.

10:30 PM to 11:00 PM ... FLOOR SHOW
Somethin' Smith & The Redheads' second show.

11:00 PM ... FUN, SPORT & AMUSEMENT
At eleven o'clock, The Dugout will be closed to the public. It will be devoted to your exclusive use.

11:00 PM to 1:30 AM ... TWIST PARTY
prizes for the best Twisters. Also, during this period, ballplayers who have an impulse to entertain are invited to take the microphone. (P.S. Mary Lou, please put Whitey to bed early.)

1:30 AM 'til ?? ... AFTER HOURS PARTY
sandwiches, coffee and assorted beverages will be served in Room 124.

SATURDAY, FEBRUARY 2, 1963

All Morning .... SLEEP
as late as you wish. Call room service for coffee.

All Morning .... ASPIRINS
Anacin, Bufferin, Alka Seltzer, Pepto-bismal, hot and cold beer and straight shots are available in room 124.

6:00 AM to noon ... BREAKFAST
is served in The Coffee Shop. When the waitress presents you with a check, just sign your name and room number.

Ray Mantle, Mickey, and Jack Myers at Miami (Oklahoma)C.C. '55

Ray Mantle, Tom (Snake) Sturdivant, Mickey, Max Mantle (cousin), Jack Myers, and Roy Mantle in Miami (Okla.) C.C. in '55.

Southern Hills has long been considered one of the nation's finest traditional layouts. It's a tree-lined Perry Maxwell masterpiece that has played host to six majors -- the 1958 U.S. Open (won, interestingly enough, by Bolt), the 1965 U.S. Amateur, the 1970 PGA Championship, the 1977 U.S. Open, the 1982 PGA and the 1994 PGA -- plus the 1995 and 1996 PGA Tour Championship. In 2001, it again will host the U.S. Open.

A par-71, Southern Hills does not lend itself to risk. It's more a test of survival. Take a chance, and you usually get burned. Just get to the green, then get off ASAP. Rewards are slim and the wind is persistent. Despite all that, Mantle let 'er rip.

"Mostly, he just fired at the pin (flagstick)," Smith said. "He had better (course) management as he got older, like anybody would. Before that, he was wild off the tee. When he first started playing in some exhibitions, he would hit a 3-iron, instead of his driver, because he was afraid he'd kill somebody with a golf ball."

When he retired after the 1968 season, Mantle had the third-highest home run total in major league history. He hit 270 home runs on the road. Despite playing 23 fewer games at home, he hit 266 at Yankee Stadium -- that's more dingers in that park (which opened in 1923) than any other player, including Babe Ruth (259). Mantle hit 373 home runs from the left side, 163 from the right side and thousands more during batting practice and exhibition games. He owns the World Series record for home runs with 18.

Mantle had the same thought process in golf that he had in baseball.

Go deep.

On one occasion, he drove the green on the dogleg right, 352-yard 17th hole... on the fly

Some of his clouts were Herculean.

On the 454-yard opening hole at Southern Hills, he often hit a sand wedge for his second shot. There was the time he put his tee shot on the 405-yard 15th hole to within 30 yards of the green. On one occasion, he drove the green on the dogleg right, 352-yard 17th hole ... on the fly. To finish things off, ignoring trees to the right and a creek precariously positioned in the fairway, Mantle ignored the entire mess and cut the corner on the dogleg right, 430-yard 18th hole. He often left himself an approach of 40 or 50 yards.

"He hit the ball a long way," said 70-year-old George Matson, who has been at Southern Hills since moving from Armagh, Ireland, in 1949, working first as a painter and now as the shop manager. "A lot of times he just went over the trees. Only a long fella can do that. We've had some long hitters come through here, but Mantle ..."

Matson would then crouch into a stance, impersonating Mantle. Most extraordinary was the

Mantle grip. He had a powerful right hand. While a standard right-handed grip has the right thumb essentially pointed upward and the "V" between the right thumb and forefinger pointed toward the right shoulder, Mantle's thumbs faced at 3 o'clock.

"I never would change his grip," Smith said. "You could see all four knuckles on top of his left hand. I never changed it because he was still playing baseball. Mickey got to where he could live with it so why change it. He would go out and play well because he stayed behind the ball. He never came over the top of the ball. He didn't even have to practice. He'd go from baseball to golf with no problem at all. I was afraid (Yankees manager) Casey Stengel

would scream at him when he was playing golf a lot. Mickey thought of Casey like his second father. And Casey just absolutely adored Mickey."

In 1962, the Smith-Mantle tandem had lost an 18-hole match at Southern Hills and were about to play an "emergency nine" when some photographers and reporters approached Mantle near No. 1 tee. Given the circumstances, it was bad timing. "Mickey wasn't in a great mood when he saw them, so he said, 'Get the hell out of here. We're playing some more golf and I just don't want to bother with you right now,' " Smith explained.

The media then explained their reason for being there. Mantle had just been selected Most Valuable Player for the third time in his career.

"Mickey flashes this big ol' smile and says, 'Well, hell, come on over,' " Smith said.

Mantle and Smith teamed to win the 1965 member-guest at Southern Hills. They each won a black and white leather golf bag. "Somebody immediately went up to Mickey and offered him $500 for the

Ralph Terry (Yankee MVP of the '56 Word Series), Dave Dennis, and Mickey at the late fall of '56, Independence (Kansas) C.C.

bag," Smith said. "Mick said, 'Hell, no. I've never won a golf tournament in my life.' "

There are stories out of Miami -- Oklahoma, not Florida.

Dr. W.D. Jackson is a retired dentist who practiced in Miami from 1951-94. A member at Miami Golf & Country Club, Jackson often played golf with Mantle's twin brothers, Roy and Ray. He also had a chance to experience Mickey.

"I barely knew him. I only got to play with him a few times, but we played in the early 1960s when he was in his prime," Jackson recalled. "We always played in the winter. It was cold and the ball didn't carry very far."

Except when you're Mickey Mantle.

The second hole at Miami Country Club is a 420-yard dogleg right lined with trees. "Mickey hit this one drive over the trees and, so help me God, I thought he popped it up," Jackson said.

After walking through the trees, Mantle's ball was discovered 5 yards short of the green. "Nobody ever dreamed of trying to drive that green," Jackson said. "That ball had to carry probably 350 yards to clear those trees."

At the 556-yard 10th hole, Mantle easily cleared a grass bunker (actually a small hill that runs across the fairway) 290 yards off the tee. "He

Mickey thought of Casey like his second father. And Casey just absolutely adored Mickey

flew it like it wasn't even there," Jackson said. "Then he reached the green with a 7-iron."

Remember, this was winter in Oklahoma, the state of extremes; where it's either extremely hot or extremely cold; where it can't decide whether it wants to rain or snow, so it does both, resulting in ice. But it is always -- always -- windy. Rodgers and Hammerstein weren't bluffing when they wrote the musical "Oklahoma!" The wind does come sweeping down the plain.

Jackson repeated a familiar story of the 391-yard fourth hole at Twin Hills in Joplin, Mo. It was there where Mantle's tee shot found the right greenside bunker.

"It didn't find the bunker," Smith countered. "It found the green. In fact, he drove that green twice in the same day."

"Ray (Mantle) once told me, 'I can't play golf with Mickey. He just destroys me,' " Jackson said. "He once said, and of course it's not true, but he once said, 'Mickey can reach any par-5 with a driver and a wedge. I don't care how long the hole is.' In my mind, I thought he could hit a 5-iron about 240 yards."

Running back Steve Owens was born and raised in Miami, just 5 miles south of Mantle's hometown of Commerce. He first met Mantle during charity golf events in the early 1970s. But in the

Local Boys; Mickey and Steve Owens, the '69 Heisman Trophy Winner.

20-plus years Owens knew Mantle, never -- not once -- did he get to play a round with the Commerce Comet.

"Mickey used to to tell Steve, 'You're just not good enough yet. Come back when you can play,' " Smith explained.

Just like Berra had told Mantle in 1955.

"Mickey saying that was incentive for me to get better," said Owens, who chopped his handicap in half (from a 20-22 to the 10-11 range) in less than a year with Smith as his teacher. "I'm not so sure I wanted to play with him, though. They (Mantle and Smith) gambled for a lot of money. They were too rich for my blood."

Throughout his life, Mantle played golf with plenty of familiar names. There were entertainers like Bob Hope and Jerry Lewis, former Detroit Lions quarterback/drinking buddy Bobby Layne and Don Meredith, plus several PGA Hall of Famers such as Sam Snead, Jack Nicklaus, Arnold Palmer, Jimmy Demaret and Lee Trevino. "He played once or twice in the Bing Crosby (at Pebble Beach), but never did enjoy it that much," Smith said. "Mickey

Mickey sitting in a '49 Plymouth convertable at the '94 Shangri-La Golf Tournament.

enjoyed playing where nobody would bother him.

Former All-Star first baseman Steve Garvey played alongside Mantle once. "Big hitter," Garvey said with a smile. "Big hitter on the field and on the links, too."

"There was this one story about the time Mickey played Lanny Wadkins," Smith said. "Lanny had just won the (1977) PGA. He came back and Mickey won $2,300 from him. He convinced Lanny to give him two drives and two putts. Mickey tore him up. When I was playing, Lanny said, 'I didn't know if I had won enough money winning the PGA Championship ($45,000) because Mantle was going to hustle me out of it.' "

Eventually, Mickey and his son Mickey would take on Marshall and his son, Marshall Jr.

"We had some knock-down, drag-out games, that's for sure," Marshall Sr. said.

"On the golf course, he wasn't obnoxious or anything. He just kind of concentrated. He was really focused," said Marshall Jr., now an assistant golf pro at Shangri-La. "Dad and I wanted to beat them as much as they wanted to beat us."

As for Mantle's swing, "I had played with guys about his age," Marshall Jr. said. "I remember times when he'd hit and, gosh, he'd knock it so far. What I remember most, though, is when he got out of the cart or had to walk. I remember his knees. I mean, he practically had to crawl to the ball. His forearms were still muscle-toned and a little carved. He had this big upper body, real strong. Then you'd look at his knees and his thighs ... I'm telling you, I had this weird feeling."

A golf course was Mantle's sanctuary. He could relax, be himself and have a good time there. He was in hiding, yet outdoors at the same time. He also formed friendships there.

"We played with (Mantle's former Yankee teammate) Roger Maris at a resort north of Orlando (Fla.)," Smith said. "We'd play golf and fish and stay a week, every year. You know, Mickey was never really close to Roger until after baseball, even though they roomed together. He remembered the times when Roger tried to horn in on fly balls hit between them in the outfield. I think Mickey in some ways resented Roger. They eventually wound up being good friends." (When Maris died of cancer on Dec. 14, 1985, Mantle was noticeably shaken and served as a pallbearer.)

Mantle often would sign his scorecard with a self-proclaimed moniker. His favorite pen name was Mickey "Little Ben" Mantle, as in Ben Hogan.

Golf would consume the remainder of Mantle's life until he died of liver cancer in August of 1995. And in the end, Mantle was more than qualified to play with his Yankee teammates.

"Yogi told Mickey he learned so fast he ought to start taking up golf seriously," Smith said. "I don't disagree. Mickey was a remarkable athlete. He could play any sport he wanted, and been darn good."

'92 Golf Tournament at Shangri-La.

LEAVING THE SCENE

As Marshall Smith drove through the streets of Commerce, he drove on instinct.

There were no signs to guide you to 319 South Quincy Street, where Mickey Mantle lived when the family first moved into town. There was no landmark revealing the house he bought for his parents after his rookie season in 1951, nor for the first house he and his wife, Merlyn, had built. There weren't street signs at every corner. In fact, many side streets were unmarked. The only way to know you were on Quincy Street was to actually know Quincy Street.

Smith knew. First a left, then a right, then another left and, presto, there stood the Mantle's first Commerce home -- sort of. Some paint and new siding has been applied, but the house's foundation was noticeably decayed. The detached garage looked frail. Out front, a mailbox bearing no name and the number 319 was mounted on a chain-link fence, facing leftward rather than for-

Galvanized steel barn used by Mickey for his many practice sessions with his father.

ward. The trees looked healthy and sturdy. A near-by barn made of sheet metal did not, however.

Yankee Stadium was the house Ruth built. This was the house Mickey Mantle nearly destroyed. He had pounded countless baseballs within these restricted confines. He caused damage with his throwing and with his hitting. "The garage and the house withstood a lot of punishment, I'll tell you," Mantle once said.

After his shift as a shoveler in the Blue Goose Number One lead and zinc mine, Mutt Mantle

would return home around 4 p.m and immediately play ball with his first son. When Mickey's talents quickly outgrew the confines surrounding the house, they ventured to a nearby cow pasture to practice ... and practice ... and practice.

Directly across the street from the old Mantle house, a pint-sized dwelling was much closer to its original state. It was scarred, sagging, and sitting on concrete blocks. Next to it sat a pile of rusted steel and rubble, a junk yard of very little worth. Compared to that, the Mantle estate

Baseball diamond in Commerce, Oaklahoma with Chat pile in the background.

seemed opulent.

Nine months before Mickey Mantle's death, a collector purchased the Quincy house for $60,500. "Mickey didn't think the place was worth $500, much less that kind of money," Smith said. The new home owner reportedly planned to move the house to Las Vegas or Branson, Mo., and re-open it as a home for Mantle memorabilia.

Commerce officials intended to build a Mickey Mantle museum at one time. Because of the poor local economy, however, the mission stalled with $30,000 in the bank. The project is still pending.

Smith drove on, continuing to follow his instincts. The other two Mantle homes on River and Maple streets appeared to be solid. Smith drove past the football field where he first met Mantle. Eventually, Smith arrived at the city's main artery.

The road which dissects Commerce carries three identities:

1) U.S. Highway 69.

Mickey and his father Mutt talk to a fellow miner outside Commerce, Oklahoma ore mine in '49

2) Route 66. The historic 2,400-mile stretch of road that connected Chicago to Santa Monica, Calif.

3) Mickey Mantle Boulevard.

Route 66 road signs have long been collectors' items. So too are the blue street signs with the white lettering, "Mickey Mantle Blvd."

Asked how many Mantle street signs have been pilfered through the years, a Commerce city official responded, "Gosh, there's no telling. A lot."

The local volunteer fire department began selling the street signs for $20 apiece -- $24 by mail. A few months after Mantle's death, however, city officials curtailed sales. Roughly 1,100 signs had been sold to the public, but it had become a bit annoying. Many purchasers were collectors who hoped the signs would appreciate in value. "That's not why we're selling them," the city official said. "We hoped people would buy them to remind them of Mickey and the time he spent here."

Commerce is flat and dry. But along with the

nearby towns of Picher, Cardin and Quapaw, there lies the Chat mountain range. Chat is spent ore, and these towns serve as graveyards for the huge piles of the worthless, unattractive rocks. "Under a leaden sky," Mantle described, "the whole area looks as barren as a wasteland: desolate, forgotten, nobody within hailing distance."

Smith meandered his way through the streets in each town. Several streets were unmarked. Many seemingly started from nowhere and ended at the base of yet another massive chat pile. Nestled between two chat mountains was a baseball field, complete with lights, bleachers and a pint-sized press box. Store signs needed a fresh coat of paint, each victimized by the countless dust storms. Not only did this vicinity endure the Depression, it also is Dust Bowl territory.

"Some of the finest people in the country live here,'" Smith said of far northeast Oklahoma. "They don't have much, but I will say this: They pay their bills on time."

Chat pile

Smith was wrong. This place is not 1,540 miles from New York City. It's at least a million miles away.

"People wonder if it was a big adjustment for Mickey to go from here to New York City," Smith said. "What do you think?"

The greater Commerce metro area essentially entails most of the civilization of Ottawa County, with its total population of 30,561.

According to the census bureau, only seven towns in Ottawa County were incorporated in 1940. They were: Miami (pop. 8,345), Picher (5,848), Commerce (2,422), Quapaw (1,054), Fairland (786); North Miami (393) and Peoria (227). Places such as Cardin, Whitebird, Dauthat, Zincville, Lincolnville and Hockerville existed, but there was no documentation of their populations.

Fifty years later, these towns boasted populations of 13,142 in Miami; 2,426 in Commerce; 1,714 in Picher; 450 in North Miami; while Cardin had 165.

Pump house in Cardin, Oklahoma.

Smith Insurance Agency founded in '17. Quapaw, Oklahoma.

Boarded-up buildings in Picher, Oklahoma

Cover of Joplin, Missouri Holiday Inn brochure. The only Holiday Inn ever named after a person.

Overcrowding is not a problem in Commerce. It never has been. From 1940 to 1990, there was a population boom of four people. From here, Mantle would venture to New York City, a quaint little village of 7.3 million people where a soldout Yankee Stadium offered a population base 23 times the size of Commerce.

"Can you imagine coming from here to playing there?" Smith said as he drove down yet another dead-end street in Picher.

Following the 1952 season, in which the Yankees beat the Brooklyn Dodgers 4 games to 3 in the World Series, Commerce threw a party for its hometown boy, who was then barely 21 years old. Wrote Mantle:

The main drag was glistening under bright lights as district bands and drum corps from all over Ottawa County marched along. Merlyn and I were in the back seat of an open convertible, waving at the crowds. Literally hundreds lined the sidewalks to give me a hero's welcome.

That night they staged a banquet at the old

Whitey Ford looks over Mickey's shoulder at the ribbon cutting ceremony of the Mickey Mantle Holiday Inn, Joplin, Missouri.

Spartan Cafeteria. My family and friends were pretty excited. I made a brief speech -- three words of thanks. Then I sat on the dais with my former high school coach, Barney Barnett, Yankees scout Tom Greenwade, Allie Reynolds, my mom, Roy and Ray, Barbara, little Butch, and Merlyn. I felt more than grateful. I was so damn proud of them all. If only my father could've been there.

... This was special. I was young and somehow it meant the world. How many times can you feel the same intensity as the first time?

After all the notoriety in New York, though, things hadn't changed much in Oklahoma, aside from the Spartan Cafeteria banquet. Total strangers in Commerce, who had never given me a second glance, were behaving like old buddies. I suddenly discovered some "close" relatives I'd never even heard of before.

Afterword, for the most part, life returned to normal. I remember running into a distant relative from Spavinaw one day.

"Hey, you're Mickey Mantle, one of Mutt's boys, right?"

"Yeah ..."

"Well, what you been doing these days?"

"I've been with the Yankees for two years."

"You don't say."

Just like I'd been working in the mines all along!

So with all this adoration, this feeling of gratitude, this "special" feeling, why did Mantle do it.

Mickey at the Holiday Inn in Joplin, Missouri, in November '61.

Why did he leave Commerce?

"People were knocking at their door all hours of the night, wanting to borrow money," Smith said. "They'd come over and use their bathroom. Can you believe that? People just wouldn't leave them alone."

After winning the Triple Crown in 1956 (leading the league in batting average, home runs and RBI's), Mantle was bombarded with various endorsement offers. Frank Scott, Mantle's agent at the time, created Mickey Mantle Enterprises. Mantle did radio and television commercials,

Mickey in an exuberant mood on April 15, '64 after rain cancelled a Boston Red Sox game at Yankee Stadium. Roger Maris is catching with Marshall Smith at bat.

made appearances, signed autographs, shook hands, attended banquets, et al. A handful of business ventures were profitable for Mantle. Most, however, were disastrous.

"I was only 25 years old, getting a little cocky -- also grossing up to about $75,000 in outside income and figuring there was no telling how much I would make by the time I was 30," Mantle wrote. "I guess it showed, because a lot of relatives and friends came to my door, saying, 'Listen, can you lend me a thousand or so?' They assumed I had it, could afford it and wouldn't turn them away. Consequently, there were many borrowers and I knew they'd never pay me back."

Mantle also was tired of the constant travel. Back then, it was almost a three-hour drive from Commerce to the Tulsa airport -- six hours round-trip, not counting the air time needed to reach his final destination.

A man named W.O. Bankston called one day, wanting to know if Mantle would be interested in taking over a bowling alley in Dallas. Bankston said bowling was all the rage, the fastest-growing indoor sport of all-time. "This is it, Mick," Bankston said, "Dallas is ripe for the picking."

All Mantle would have to do was move to Dallas and allow Bankston to name the alley after Mantle.

The change would ease Mantle's traveling woes immensely. He already had a successful venture with Harold Youngman at the new Mickey Mantle Holiday Inn in Joplin, Mo. Youngman warned Mantle against the bowling alley deal. After doing brisk business initially, the alley went out of buisness within a few years.

Billy Martin making dinner, "Italian Style," at Marshall Smiths' Home in Miami, Okla.

"I simply wanted to prove I could do pretty well on my own, which I couldn't," Mantle admitted. "I should've stayed put in Commerce ... but all that is water under the bridge."

When the Mantle phenomenon returned to Commerce during the off-season, he often was suffocated. Everyone was his friend, especially the people he couldn't remember ever meeting. If such was the case, no one hesitated to try and refresh his memory.

"We were in the second grade together."

"We met once in junior high."

"We had the same high school teacher."

"We once bumped in to each other in the food line."

"I sat directly behind you in the movie theater, don't you remember?"

Suddenly, everyone resembled Chris Farley's Hollywood critic character on "Saturday Night Live."

"Hey, uh, remember that time when you were a rookie and your team won the World Series. You had to watch it from your hospital bed because

Micky and Frank Crosetti in the Yankee dugout. August '61.

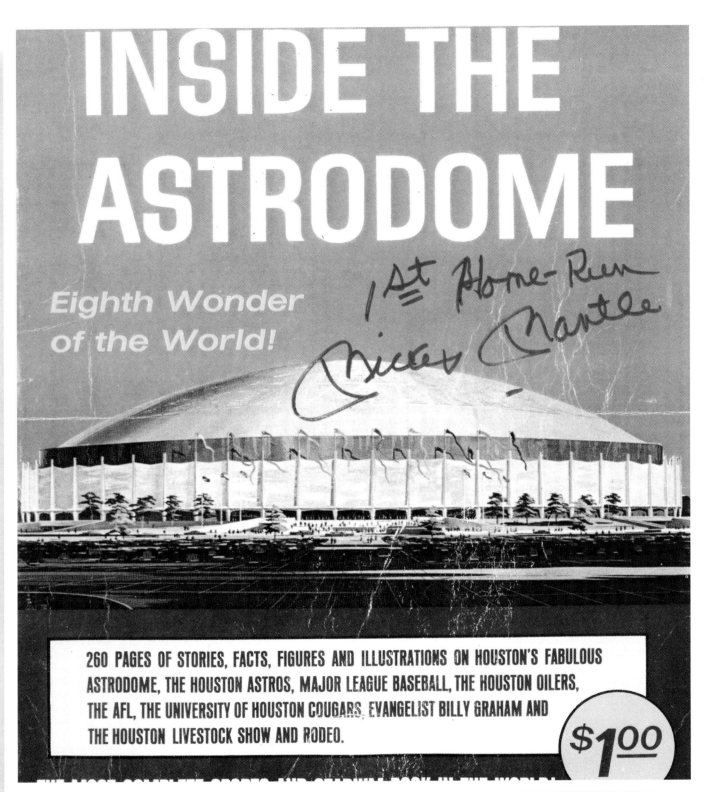

Mickey hit the first home run in the Houston Astrodome.

you hurt your leg on that sprinkler head. Your dad was in the same hospital room with you when he was really sick? Huh, do ya remember that? ... Yeah, me too ... Oh, remember that one time you crashed into the outfield fence? Did that hurt? ... Yeah, that was neat ...''

"He'd try to be humble," Smith said of Mantle. "But then they'd start on that Do you remember this? Do you remember that? If Mickey couldn't remember something, they'd get mad at him, called him arrogant, or a jerk, or worse. People wouldn't see him in 20 years and then when Mickey didn't recognize them, they'd call him a horse's ass. How fair is that?"

People wouldn't see him in 20 years and then when Mickey didn't recognize them, they'd call him a horse's ass

"I thought he treated almost everybody great overall. But when he was drinking, he'd get tough and rough. He didn't get into fights or anything like that. He'd usually be the one trying to calm everybody down. Nobody ever really challenged Mickey to a fight, and I don't blame them. With his reflexes, I think he could have been a great boxer."

Inside nearly every store or business near Commerce, you could find some sort of Mantle shrine. For a man who allegedly didn't want to sign many autographs, a lot of town people sure have them.

If anyone could relate to Mantle's three-ring circus at home, it's hometown hero Steve Owens, who grew up in nearby Miami.

Was there ever a time things got so hectic Owens wanted to leave the state?

"Not really," said Owens, who resides in Norman, roughly 230 miles to the southwest. "Of course, Commerce is a lot smaller than Miami (roughly one-sixth the size).

"I didn't really get annoyed, but sometimes I'd want to spend time with my mom and dad and brothers and sisters. It seemed like every time I went back there, somebody would call and want to do this and that. They'd see my car outside the house, come by, drop in, say they were going to stay 15 minutes, and would end up staying two hours. It was hard to do at times, but it never really got to the point where I didn't want to go back. I wasn't really upset, but you can't please everybody.

"I've really maintained my attachment to Miami. I have my golf benefit there every year at Miami Country Club (a charity event which raised more than $300,000 in its first six years). My mother, four brothers and sisters still live in Miami. I still have a strong family connection there. I always had a lot of support in Miami when I was coming up, and they're still friends of mine. Every time I go back there it still feels like home to me. I love Norman, it's a special place.

But for me, Miami's home. I always love going back there."

Long after Mantle moved away from Commerce, Smith would chauffeur the hometown hero through the same streets, on automatic pilot, driving by instinct. Rarely, if ever, would Mantle let people know he was visiting.

Smith's wife, Corinne, went along for some of those rides. "I'd be sitting in the backseat while they were in the car," she said. "You wouldn't believe some of their conversations. I wish I'd had a tape recorder with me."

"If he knew nobody was out there to take advantage, he would have gone out in public more often," Smith said. "We were driving along and he saw this man mowing his lawn and his son was watching him. He said, 'Stop the car.' He walked over to visit with them. Turns out Mick knew the child's father, but he didn't know that when we stopped the car. He gave the kid an autographed baseball. Of course, that boy probably had no idea who Mickey Mantle was. Mickey did that kind of stuff all the time. It didn't matter where we were."

Some bitter Commerce residents tried to wipe Mantle from their memories, but couldn't. When he died, reprints of old Mantle black-and-white photographs skyrocketed at local photo shops.

> "*If he knew nobody was out there just to take advantage, he would have gone out in public more often*"

Smith made several trips to New York City during and after Mantle's career. While in New York, he would go to the ballpark, join Mantle in the locker room after games, then tag along for a night on the town at, among other places, Toot Shoor's, Jack Dempsey's and the 21 Club. There also were parties in the Governor's Suite at the St. Moritz Hotel, where Mantle resided during several seasons. In terms of alcohol consumption, Smith was no competition for Mantle. "I get sick when I drink," Smith admitted. "God was good to me."

One of those trips came on opening day against Boston. The game was eventually called due to rain. During the rain delay, Smith stood in the batter's box in his dress clothes. Mantle, in full uniform, stood at the pitcher's mound, and right fielder Roger Maris played the role of catcher.

There was Smith, on the field in Yankee Stadium, with Mantle and Maris, two teammates who combined for more home runs in one season (115) than any player tandem in the history of the game.

"Can you believe that?" Smith said, shaking his head in disbelief.

As Smith stepped into the batter's box, Maris offered a warning. "You better watch out because

I'm not sure where these pitches are going. I'm serious," Maris said.

Mantle threw his bread-and-butter pitch to Smith -- the knuckleball. "You wouldn't believe what he could make that do," Smith said, laughing. "Mickey probably had as good a knuckle as any pitcher he ever faced," he said laughingly.

Mantle had casually thrown the knuckle ball during his days at Commerce High School. He began experimenting with the pitch during his first year of pro ball with the Yankees' Class D club in Independence, Kan. Prior to a game at Bartlesville, Okla., Mantle warmed up on the sidelines with third baseman Lou Skizas.

Skizas squatted down and baited Mantle. "OK. Let's see it, kid."

Mantle uncorked a knuckler that struck Skizas smack dab on the nose and sent him tumbling. Skizas was unconscious for two or three minutes and was rushed to the Bartlesville infirmary. The end result was a broken nose, three missed days of ball, and some new-found respect for Mantle's knuckler.

"Matter of fact," Mantle wrote, "he still has a permanent lump on his nose."

This was the deadly pitch Smith faced during this rare opportunity. His success was limited. "I think I hit one pitch -- barely. It was a ground ball that didn't leave the infield. That's about it," Smith said. Good news, no HBP (hit-by-pitch).

Mantle often wondered what his career home run total might have been had he played in a home park the size of Ebbets Field, home of the Brooklyn Dodgers, rather than at Yankee Stadium. Ebbets Field was 297 feet down the right-field line and 389 feet to dead-center field. Meanwhile, in those days, Yankees Stadium measured 296 down the right-field line, 344 feet to right field, 407 feet to right-center and an astounding 461 feet to straightaway center (with the flag pole and Monument Park on the warning track roughly 10 feet in front of the outfield wall).

Mantle and Whitey Ford once figured Mantle averaged 15 long outs per season in Yankee Stadium. "In my 18 years I would have gotten 270 additional home runs if I'd been a Dodger," Mantle said in *The Mick*.

The Mantle legend wouldn't have been quite the same. Remember, the Dodgers moved to Los Angeles. When Ebbets Field was torn down, so, too, would have been the Mantle Mystique, which continued to reverberate through Yankee Stadium for decades.

> **M**antle uncorked a knuckler that struck Skizas smack dab on the nose and sent him tumbling. Skizas was unconscience for two or three minutes.

*Mickey throwing his bat over the roof at Al Lang Field
during a spring training game vs. the Red Sox in March of '57.*

Smith recalled a time when he was in New York City after Mantle had retired. The Yankees were playing a World Series game and Billy Martin was their manager.

"We were in this limo, having a good time, watching the game on television," Smith said. "One of the Yankees' pitchers was getting hit pret-ty good. I don't remember his name. Anyway, Mickey couldn't believe Billy was leaving him in the game. So he said, 'I'm gonna get hold of Billy inside the dugout.' I figured the chances of him getting hold of Billy inside the dugout were slim and none. I don't know how he did it, but before I knew it, Mickey's on the phone with Billy. You could see Billy on TV, talking on the phone."

Mantle: "Why the hell are you keeping that pitcher in there? They're hitting him to death."

Martin: "You want him out of there?"

Mantle: "Hell, yes. Don't you?"

"Within one minute, Billy went out to the mound and pulled that pitcher," Smith said.

Martin was a familiar face at Smith's home. During Super Bowl weekend in 1984, Martin required a huge pot from a local restaurant so he could make five gallons of spaghetti sauce.

"Billy Martin's spaghetti sauce was as good as they make it," Corinne Smith said. "He was an artist at it. He wouldn't let me help, wouldn't let my clean up or anything. He said, 'You just stay out of this kitchen.' We froze some of that sauce. It was so good."

"One time he went to Tulsa and bought something like $153 worth of ingredients just to put in the sauce," Marshall Smith said. "Then the manager of the store came over. He wanted to know if they could put a picture of Billy on the wall in return for the food, and they did."

The Smiths are nearly as defensive about Martin as they are about Mantle.

"I think Billy Martin helped Mickey more than he hurt him," Marshall Smith said. "People were always saying Billy hurt Mickey, but that

never came from Mickey. And that'll never come from me. Billy had a lot of class. When I say class, Mickey never learned how to present himself in public. Billy could absolutely drag you into loving him. Mickey couldn't. Billy used to chew out Mickey all the time about not giving autographs. One thing about Billy, he'd tell you what the hell he thought."

People were always saying Billy hurt Mickey, but that never came from Mickey

Mantle was no Joe DiMaggio, not even close. Because of his osteomyelitis, Mantle was classified as 4-F numerous times and did not serve in the military and many fans resented it. He was a foreigner from a foreign land -- Oklahoma. He was surly to the media and often surly to the public, particularly with persistent autograph seekers. His inner circle was very small, very tight.

Because of these reasons and many more, Mantle was not readily accepted for several seasons at the outset of his career. This being New York, it was not difficult to detect. Hate mail came in droves. Cheers came only with home runs. Boos came with every strikeout.

"Those days hurt Mickey, they hurt him a lot," Smith said.

"For whatever reason, who knows why he was treated like that?" said Bobby Murcer, an Oklahoma native who played for the Yankees in 13 of his 17 major-league seasons. "New York fans are the greatest fans. They're also the toughest fans. They hold their legends high. They aren't quick to accept new players moving in on a legend's territory."

Murcer said the comparisons between Mantle and DiMaggio shouldn't have occurred in the first place. "You can't compare the players, can't compare the times," Murcer said. "You can't compare those times to these. It's silly to try."

Rudy Riska is the Executive Director of the Heisman Memorial Trophy Trust at the Downtown Athletic Club in New York City. He was a right-handed pitcher for the Yankees' organization (1954-58) and reached as high as the Triple-A level.

"I'm the kind of guy who looks into a person's psyche and I always thought Mickey was a good person," Riska said. "Sadly, though, he was always a rube. He was a good-natured farm boy who hung around with people who took advantage of him. He was never accepted here, at first, because he had to replace DiMaggio. People were behind DiMaggio then and would never let that happen. Slowly, they began to accept him, but there were so many strikeouts and so many tantrums in between. I remember one time Casey Stengel grabbed him and shook him after he had spilled over a water cooler. Casey just grabbed

him and shook him down the steps, right there in the dugout.

"I liked Mickey. Toward the end we got friendly in the sense he came down for the (Bicentennial) Fourth of July party here. We spent about four hours together, looking at the ships and everything. I went to his golf tournament at Shangri-La (in Oklahoma). I really wasn't all that close to him. I have more stories with DiMaggio than Mickey. But I liked him. I really thought he was a genuine person underneath. You scratch away the other stuff, he was a good-hearted guy, you know."

Casey just grabbed him and shook him down the steps, right there in the dugout

Not all of Smith's road trips were to New York. There were several to Chicago and to spring training in St. Petersburg, Fla.

Smith was on hand when Mantle hit the first-ever home run in the Houston Astrodome during an exhibition game against Baltimore in 1965. Of course, there would be several other mighty clouts.

During his season with the Class C Joplin Miners, Mantle hit so many home runs toward an orphans' home behind the right-field fence that a bedsheet soon appeared with a message: "Thanks for the ball, Mickey!" One time, Mantle hit a ball deep over the center-field fence. The team's veteran equipment manager greeted Mantle in the dugout by saying, "That's the longest homer I've seen since Babe Ruth cleared Sportsman's Park roof back in the '28 World Series."

On April 10, 1953, Mantle hit a home run over the 100-foot high grandstands during an exhibition game at Forbes Field in Pittsburgh. Until then, only Ruth and Ted Beard had done it. All this after Mantle, Martin and Ford paid a $500 cab fare from Cincinnati to Pittsburgh after missing the team train. Mantle arrived shortly before game time, didn't take batting practice, hit the long homer during his first at-bat, then was given the rest of the game off.

One week later, on April 17, Mantle hit one out of Griffith Stadium in Washington against Chuck Stobbs. Some said it was the longest home run ever hit in the majors. Measuring 565 feet, it cleared the back bleacher wall by 60 feet, grazed the corner of a huge scoreboard, and came to rest in the back yard of a private home a block away. Newspapers went nuts the next day with maps, diagrams and arrows showing where the ball left the park, how high and where it landed.

Incredibly, in the Yanks' very next game, in St. Louis against the Browns, Mantle crushed a home run at Sportsman's Park that some witnesses claim might have traveled even farther. Because of all the attention the previous monster had received, this one was never measured, never publicized.

And in 1963 there was Mantle's blast against

Bill Fischer of the Kansas City Athletics that missed clearing the right-field facade at Yankee Stadium by a mere 18 inches -- 367 feet to the spot where it hit; 108 feet, 1 inch to fall to the earth. One engineer estimated it would take a clout of 620 feet to clear the roof at Yankee Stadium. Mantle had missed by a foot-and-a-half.

"To tell the truth, I've long forgotten how far most of those home runs went," Mantle wrote. "In fact, I've forgotten half the stuff they've written about me -- that is, the home runs and the distances. I mean, Stan Musial and Ted Williams were both every bit as strong as I am. The difference is they were always trying to meet the ball while I was always trying to kill it. If you swing for distance, you almost have to have the bat in motion before the pitch is even released. You can't chop at it and expect it to go 500 feet. You take a full cut and generate a little extra power, praying you don't miss."

Although proud of his accomplished power and acceptant of his propensity for striking out, Mantle was far more distressed about one particular statistic.

His final batting average was .298. He hated the fact it dipped below .300. In the final three seasons, he hit a combined .254 with a career-low .237 his final year in 1968. Had Mantle collected 17 more hits in his career -- less than one hit per

After baseball, Smith and Mantle kept what they called a "scratch list"

season -- he would have retired as a .300 hitter.

After baseball, Smith and Mantle kept what they called a "scratch list." Get on that list and don't expect any favors.

"We listed the people we thought weren't true-blue," Smith said. "Sometimes Mickey would call me and say take that guy off the scratch list because we're back together. He had a heart of gold. There was a long scratch list, and a short list of those you could trust."

Boston relief pitcher Dick Radatz was on the scratch list.

Smith: "What the devil you got him on the list for?"

Mantle: "He struck me out 43 times."

"We took him off the list," Smith said with a smile.

Pitcher Warren Spahn was a longtime occupant on the scratch list. His crime? Refusing to sign an autograph for longtime Mantle friend Darrell Royal and being rude in the process.

Smith admits Mantle and he went their separate ways at one time. "It was for about two years," Smith said. "He and I were in this business deal together and I told him the guy who was running it was a crook. Well, he was a friend of Mickey's and he got real upset. A few years later, the business was under investigation and Mickey could have gone to jail over it."

> *His crime? Refusing to sign an autograph for longtime friend Darrell Royal, and being rude in the process*

Mantle was a frequent visitor to the Smith house. How many visits?

"A ton," Smith said.

One time, Marshall Jr. and his friend, Matt Brady, were sitting at a table inside the Smith residence in Miami. Mantle opened the door and walked inside:

Mantle: "Hey, Little Mott. Are your mom and dad here?"

Little Marshall: "No, they're not here right now, Mickey."

Mantle walked over to a small refrigerator and took out a beer.

Mantle: "Well, tell 'em I dropped by and I'll see them a little later."

Mantle departed.

Brady (drop-jawed): "Marshall, that was Mickey Mantle."

Marshall: "Yeah, I know. He comes by every so often, but I really don't like visiting with him when he's been drinking."

Was Mantle led down a destructive path with alcoholism, or did he choose that road on his own? Had Mantle spent more time with, say, future lay minister Bobby Richardson rather than with other teammates, would things have been different?

"I think he might have still lived that same life," Marshall Sr. said. "I couldn't say that for sure, though."

Mickey displays the ball after his 1,000th hit during a game against the Washington Senators in July of '57.

MICKEY'S YANKEE
SCRAPBOOK

This is not a book about baseball. This is a book about friendship. For nearly half a century, Marshall Smith befriended Mickey Mantle, a blue-eyed blond from Oklahoma who just happened to become the most powerful switch-hitter in the history of major league baseball.

There were: 536 career home runs; a .298 lifetime batting average; a record 2,041 games as a Yankee; 1,734 walks; 1,710 strikeouts; 16 All-Star games; 12 American League pennants; seven World Series rings; three Most Valuable Player awards; the magical year of 1956 that included the Triple Crown, Hickock Belt and Silver Bat; and the Gold Glove in 1962.

Fans knew Mickey Mantle by the numbers.

Marshall Smith knew Mickey Mantle by the heart.

Books about Mantle have been written and rewritten. Naturally, because Mantle was who he was, baseball often will be used as a point of reference.

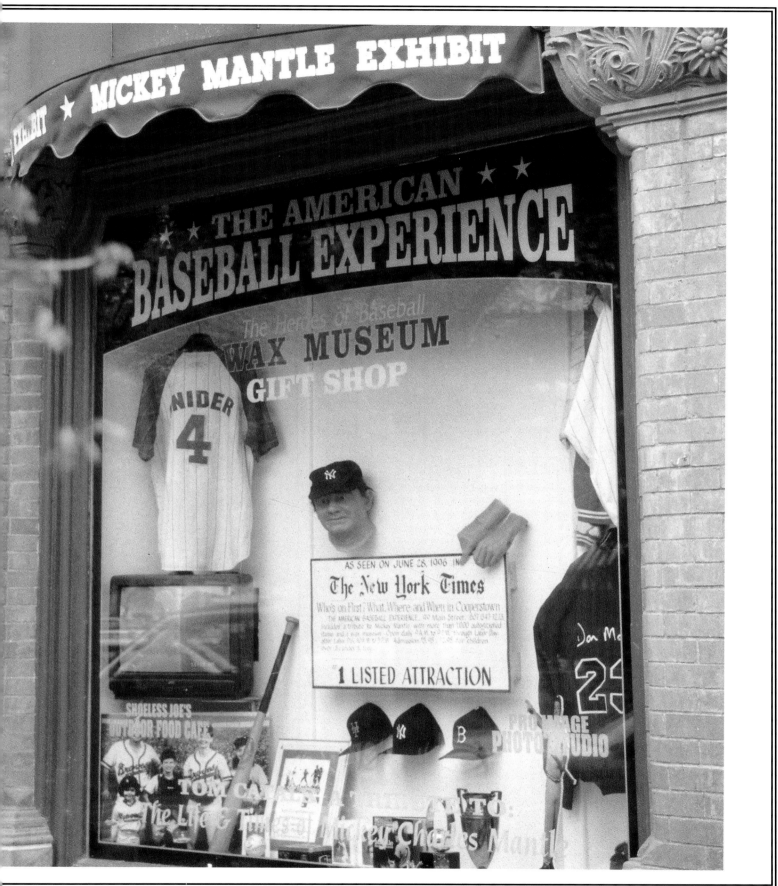

Mickey reading a letter, from his dad, inside the Yankee locker room in '51.

Mickey and Joe D., '51.

Joe DiMaggio, Mickey and Ted Williams, 51.

Joe DiMaggio, Mickey and Ted Williams, 51.

Mickey at Spring training wearing #6; his first season with the Yankees in '51.

Mickey connecting for a home run during his rookie season.

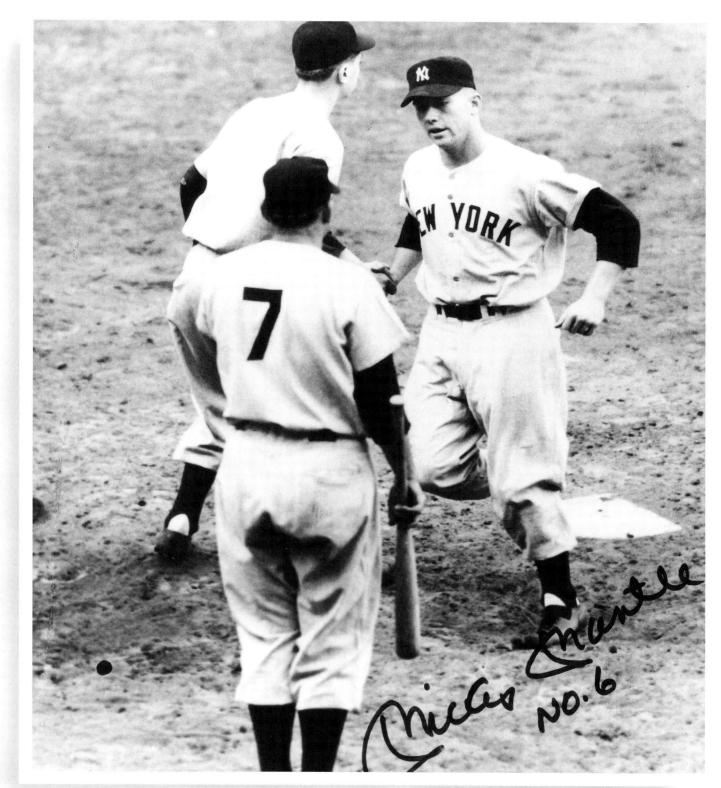

Mickey crossing home plate after hitting a home run; waiting to congratulate him is #7 Cliff Mapes, '51.

Mickey on the cover of the June '56 Sports Illustrated Magazine.
This is the year that Mickey won the Triple Crown.

Mickey being congratulated by: Tom Tresh (#15), Joe Pepitone (#25), Elston Howard (#32), and Frank Crosetti as he crosses home plate during the '67 World Series.

Casey Stengel disputes a call while Mickey awaits his turn at bat, '57.

Casey Stengel, Lee McPhail and George Weiss look on as Mickey signs his 1st $100,000 contract, February '63.

Mickey with his idol Stan "The Man" Musial, '58.

Mickey with manager Casey Stengel after winning the '56 Triple Crown Award.

Stan Musial, Mickey and Joe DiMaggio, '63.

Mickey breaking up a double play attempt against PeeWee Reese (Brooklyn Dodgers) in the '56 World Series.

Ted Williams, Yogi Berra and Mickey together at the All-Star Game, '58

Mickey and Hank Aaron at Yankee Stadium in the '58 World Series.

*Mickey pointing to the torn baseball cover from his 565 foot home run ball
he hit on April 17, 1953 against Chuck Stobbs of the Washington Senators.*

Roger Maris and Mickey; the M&M Boys,' '61.

Article from the New York Mirror Magazine, May 12, 1963 casting Mantle and Maris in the mold of 6 other Yankee greats who are all enshrined in the Baseball Hall of Fame.

Mantle and Maris autographed 8 x 10's; the M&M Boys gave fans a real treat in '61 chasing Babe Ruth's home run record of 60 in a single season. Mantle hit 54 and Maris broke the record with 61.

Joe
McCarthy

NEW YORK

PEREZ

Joe McCarthy.
Mickey Mantle will always
play. If he can

Written in '62 by Yankee managerial great Joe McCarthy: His feelings describing Mickey's attitude toward playing baseball.

The first Mickey Mantle day held on September 18, 1965 in Yankee Stadium.
Looking on (to the left) are his wife Merlyn, son Mickey Jr., and Robert Kennedy.

Mickey hitting a home run from the left side.

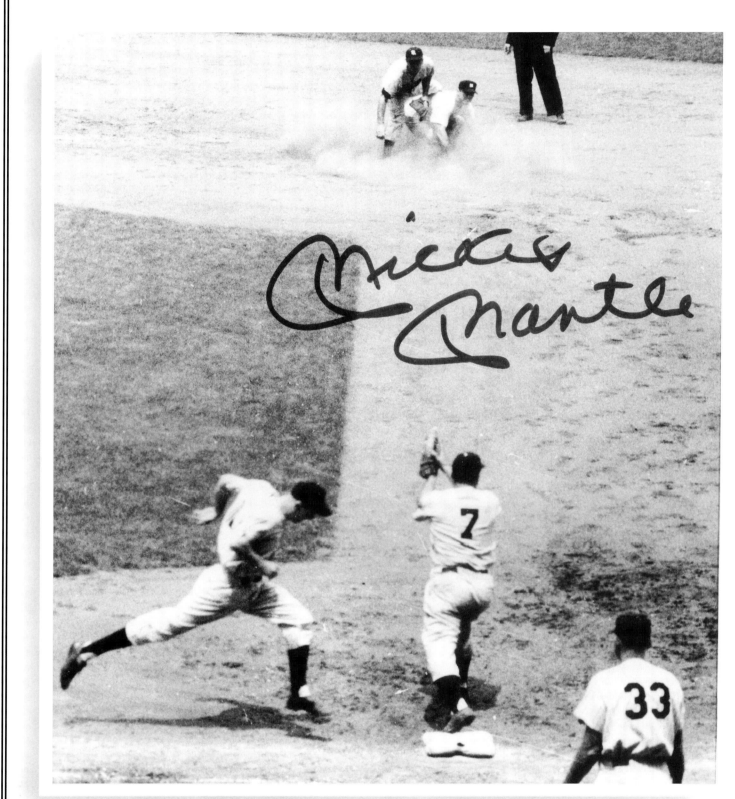

Mickey playing 1st base during his last year in baseball, '68.

Mickey was presented a set of golf clubs by Milwaukee fans in '68. It was the first time Mickey had played there since the '58 World Series. The Yankees beat the Chicago White Sox, 5-4 but Mickey went hitless in 5 trips to the plate.

*Yogi Berra, Hank Bauer (the proud father) and Mickey look at a
picture of Charlene Bauer and her newborn son Herman, '56.*

Three teammates (from the old days) get together before the New York Yankees / Oakland Athletics game at Yankee Stadium, April 15, 1958. They are: Whitey Ford, now coaching for the Yanks, former slugger Joe DiMaggio, currently a coach for the A's, and Mickey Mantle, still active as first baseman for New York.

Mickey sliding into 3rd base against Baltimore Orioles Hall of Famer Brooks Robinson. Was he safe or out? According to Mickey he was 'Safe.' According to Brooks he was 'Out.'

Roger Maris, Willie Mays and Mickey before the start of the '61 All-Star Game.

Mickey being greeted at home plate by Yogi Berra at Doubleday Field in Cooperstown, N.Y. during the Hall of Fame Game in August '54.

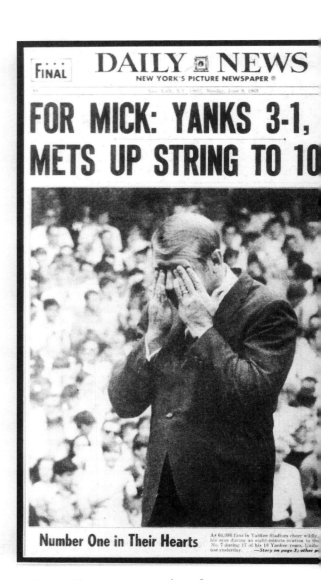

Mickey Mantle retires. June 8, 1969, Yankee Stadium.

DAILY NEWS, MONDAY, JUNE 9, 1969

Reaching out for their star, fans in the field boxes at Yankee Stadium pour forth affection for Mickey Mantle as he's ridden around the huge ballpark in a bullpen cart. Appropriately, the cart bears license number MM-7. The fans—60,096 of them—the politicians and the celebrities were on hand for the retirement of the Mick's No. 7. It now joins Babe Ruth's No. 3, Lou Gehrig's No. 4 and Joe DiMaggio's No. 5.—*Story on page 3; other picture on back page*

Mickey Mantle—A Natural

Mick and man he replaced in centerfield, Joe DiMaggio, show off plaque commemorating DiMag's exploits which will hang with one recalling Mantle's, on centerfield wall. Mick told Joe that Joe's should hang higher.

Famed pinstripe hangs in locker room as Mick

Two of the men who managed Mantle teams, Yogi Berra and Ralph Houk, race onto field for ceremony.

The man of the hour acknowledges the cheers of the faithful—like a last hurrah.

Mantle watches as clubhouse man Pete Sheehy packs away No. 7.

HERE COMES THE BRIDE

The day is June 8.

It's June 8, 1963, the day Marshall Smith and the former Corinne Hunt were married in Quapaw, Okla. It was Mantle who had convinced Smith to approach Hunt. The happy couple would occupy the second half of Mantle's 63 years.

It's June 8, 1969, the day Mickey Mantle's uniform number was retired, when he said good-bye at Yankee Stadium and received a 10-minute standing ovation. Hall of Famer Joe DiMaggio (1936-51), whom Mantle replaced in center field, formally presented Mantle with a plaque that now can be found in the famed Monument Park area beyond the outfield wall.

And it's June 8, 1995, the day Mickey Mantle had a liver transplant at Baylor University Hospital in Dallas. The 7 1/2-hour operation extended his life 66 more days, until he died of cancer that had spread to his lungs and other vital organs.

Marshall and Corinne Smith on their wedding day. June 8, '63.

The boat, "Miss Quapaw", on Grand Lake where Marshall and Corinne Smith enjoyed their honeymoon.

That line would follow Mantle for years. Oh, if the walls of the Mickey Mantle Suite could talk ...

"That kind of stuff would have to be put in a book that was rated double-R," Marshall Smith explained, stopping just shy of the NC-17 and X ratings.

"Actually, I don't think Mickey ever slept in his suite," Corinne said. "The one he always slept in was the Whitey Ford Suite. The Mickey Mantle Suite was a big room with a bar and a hideaway bed. It was more of a party room. The Whitey Ford Suite had a living room and a bedroom."

There also was the Yogi Berra Suite, which essentially was two connecting rooms with his name on the door. There was no Billy Martin Suite, however.

"Youngman never really liked Martin," Marshall said.

And many of Mantle's close friends never really liked Youngman.

Before his death in 1990, Youngman pawned numerous items Mantle had given him as gifts. Several items simply "disappeared."

"He sold Mickey's 1956 World Series ring to a collector for $8,000," Marshall said. "That guy sold it to Upper Deck for $65,000, then they sold it for $285,000."

As Marshall spoke, Samara nodded in agreement.

"We had this trophy case at the Holiday Inn that was filled with various awards Mickey had won -- the Hickock Belt, the Gold Glove, things like that," Samara said. "When we left the hotel, all the stuff had disappeared. You know who took it? Harold Youngman, that's who."

Marshall nodded and said, "That's Harold Youngman. I used to call him, 'Mr. 20 Percent.' Mickey got so mad at him, they didn't talk for years and years."

Corinne wasn't a big Youngman fan, either.

"He was a horse's butt," Corinne said. "He liked young women. He was just a womanizer. He was a nasty old man. I won't tell you what he said to me one time, but I was young and I was very embarrassed and humiliated."

Corinne had dealt with flirtation. Considering the reputation of the company she kept, it was tough not to.

"But Mickey's flirtation wasn't dirty. Harold was dirty," Corinne said. "As Mickey got older, and I got older, he started treating me like one of the boys ... Oh, man. Could he use a four-letter word. I didn't take offense at it. I thought it was kind of neat for him to accept me like that. We were all friends and he knew that."

Marshall, 15 years older than his bride-to-be, was separated from his previous wife in 1961. Mantle suggested approaching the cute young lady who worked at the front desk, Corinne Hunt.

"I'm telling you," Mantle told Marshall,

The one he always slept in was the Whitey Ford Suite

"she's made for you. Actually, she's too good for you, but you've got to meet her."

"Who?" was Marshall's response.

"Well, I knew who she was because she had always checked me into the hotel and everything," Marshall explained. "I just didn't know her name."

Meanwhile, Corinne had been given some advice from a third party. "If you want to know Mickey Mantle," she was told, "you've got to get to know Marshall Smith. They've known each other for 14 years."

There were frequent trips to Kansas City for hotel employees when the Yankees played the Athletics. Mantle would always point out single Yankees. Football great Paul Hornung, the 1956 Heisman Trophy winner out of Notre Dame, nicknamed "The Golden Boy," was at one party. "He was just passing through," Corinne said. "Of course, I thought he was just darling."

There also was Clete Boyer, that young buck via Alba High School near Joplin, and a part-time clothes salesman. "I always felt safe around Cletis," Corinne said.

Eventually, Marshall and Corinne began to chat, got to know each other and roughly one year later -- after Marshall's divorce had become final -- they began dating in October of 1962.

Mantle would invite Marshall to Dallas to play golf. Merlyn Mantle would call and invite Corinne. "Merlyn was very nice to me, very gracious," Corinne said repeatedly.

"I remember one time someone had written all over the driveway in chalk. When Mickey got upset at the children, he'd make them line up on the stair steps. At the time, the kids were 9, 7, 5 and 3. Mickey started, and went right on down the line."

Mantle: "Little Mickey, did you write on the driveway?"

Mickey Jr.: "No, daddy. I didn't do it."

Mantle: "David, did you?"

David: "No, daddy. I didn't do it."

Mantle: "Billy, did you?"

Billy: "No, I didn't do it, daddy. Danny did it."

Danny (tears flowing down both cheeks): "Daddy, I didn't do it. I don't even know how to write."

On Valentine's Day in 1963, Marshall proposed. Corinne accepted.

"Oh, well. Might as well," Corinne claimed she thought. "It was probably the closest I was ever going to get to Mickey Mantle."

Roughly one month later, Corinne quit working at the Holiday Inn. On June 8 that same year, the couple married in Marshall's mother's house.

> *There also was Clete Boyer, that young buck via Alba High School near Joplin, and a part-time clothes salesman*

The Mantles did not attend the Smith wedding. It was in the middle of baseball season. "If Mickey wouldn't have been playing baseball, I definitely would have asked him to be my best man," Marshall said. "But because it was in June, I didn't even think about it."

Ironically, a limping Mantle could have been on hand for the ceremony.

On June 5, 1963, in Baltimore, Mantle broke the instep of his left foot after catching his toe on the chain-link outfield fence while chasing down a Brooks Robinson fly ball to deep center. Mantle went home to recuperate, missed 61 games because of the injury and played just 65 total games that season, one year after winning his third MVP award.

The Smiths were married on a Saturday, then went to Grand Lake on Sunday. On Monday, Mantle telephoned from Joplin, where he was resting. "Hey, would you mind if we come down to the lake and join you on your honeymoon for a few days?" Mantle asked Marshall.

"Hell, no. We wouldn"t mind," replied Marshall, not Corinne.

Mickey, Merlyn, Marshall and Corinne spent two or three days at Grand Lake on Smith"s 32-foot cabin cruiser named Miss Quapaw. "The boat slept four, eight if you were close friends," Marshall joked. "That was a real enjoyable time for us."

The Smiths have four children, plus Elizabeth from Marshall's first marriage. The family batting order is: Corinne (yes, another one), Cathy, Christy and Marshall (yes, another one of them, too). Corinne liked the idea of naming each daughter starting with the letter C. Had Marshall Jr. been of the opposite persuasion, his (her) name would have been Cynthia.

"He would have been my little Cindy," Corinne promised. "When I got ready to go to the hospital to have Little Marshall, Cathy said, "Oh, mommy, bring me a baby brother." I almost cried because I figured there was no way I'd bring home a baby brother. But I did, and we couldn"t have been happier."

All the Smiths got to spend time with Mantle.

"Mickey was close to our kids and had a lot of respect for them," Marshall said.

"He was awfully good to our children," Corinne echoed.

"We'd be driving down the road," Marshall explained, "and Mickey would say, 'Stop the car.' We'd get out and he'd say, 'Now, Little Marshall, when you take your stance, you've got to do it like this. And you've got to be mean. You've got to hate the opponent while you're playing, even if it's your best friend.'"

There was the time Mantle went to Little Marshall's Little League practice. "All the other kids went berserk," Big Marshall said.

There was the time, at age 12, when both Marshalls joined Mantle at spring training in St.

Petersburg, Fla. They walked around the locker room, meeting the current Yankees.

"When I was 13," Marshall Jr. said, "I was on an all-star team. We were facing a pitcher who could throw really fast, and I couldn't hit him. Dad called Mickey and he told me -- and it was probably the only batting rule I remember -- 'Against a fastball pitcher, stand behind the plate as far as you can. Get a longer look at the ball. Wait on it as much as you possibly can.'" Little Marshall, who was born in 1969, lost interest in baseball around age 14 to concentrate solely on golf.

"The times I remember most about Mr. Mantle were just sitting around, one on one, just being himself," Marshall Jr. said. "I never really knew who he was. I just thought of him as dad's friend, Mickey Mantle."

Little Marshall's exposure to Mantle's remarkable talent has been limited to commercials and videotapes.

When Mantle became ill shortly before his death, Marshall Jr., was working for his step-sister Elizabeth's motion picture catering service in California. "I remember listening to this radio station and getting an update on how his health was," Little Marshall said. "And it was a younger-aged

Billy Martin and Marshall, Jr. share a baseball moment.

station. That's when I began to realize, 'God, this guy was really, really famous.' I don't think I had realized it before.

"Since he's passed away, everything I see on Mickey Mantle I try to study and find out about him, how good a player he was," Marshall Jr. said. "I never knew that many stats or records or anything like that, but now I realize he was among a select few."

SIGN HERE PLEASE

In 1987, on a flight from Albany, N.Y., to Dallas, Mickey Mantle felt a pain in his chest and was unable to breathe. He located a stewardess and asked if she had ever dealt with a passenger who was having a heart attack. The flight attendent administered oxygen to Mantle, who was pale and sweating. Mantle insisted he wasn't drunk and wasn't battling a hangover. "I just ran out of gas," he explained.

When the plane touched down at Love Field, an ambulance was waiting. While Mantle was being wheeled away on a stretcher, a man walked up and asked for an autograph.

"Little Mickey almost whipped the guy," explained Mantle's friend, Marshall Smith. "He had to tell the paramedics to pull him (the autograph seeker) away."

Turns out Mantle had not suffered a heart attack on that flight. It was only a scare. Mantle admitted that if indeed it were a heart attack, "I've

Mickey signing baseballs at his '93 golf tournament in Oklahoma.

The crowds line up for a Mickey autograph at his golf tournament at Shangri-La Resort in Afton, Oklahoma, '92.

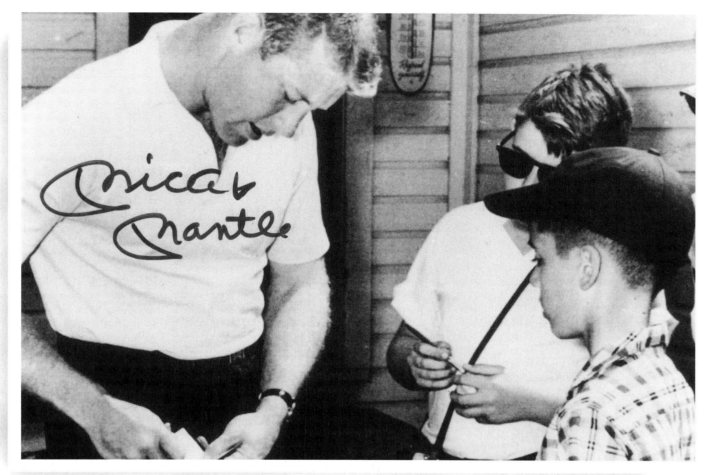

Mickey takes a moment to sign autographs for anxious fans.

been having them all my life."

During his annual charity golf tournament at the Shangri-La Resort in northeast Oklahoma, Mantle would sign autographs until he got writer's cramp. Eventually, the autograph session would have to be cut off. An announcement was read over the clubhouse public address system: "Mr. Mantle will not be available for any more autographs. We appreciate your cooperation."

Mantle was in the men's room, tending to business. Within seconds, a hand carrying a base-ball appeared above the stall door. "Hey, Mick, could you sign this baseball for me? Actually, it's not for me. It's for my neice. Her name is Bob."

"Mickey said he used two hands to sign the ball while he was going to the bathroom, but I know he's lyin' on that deal," Smith said with a laugh. "That kind of stuff happened to him all the time."

Once, after visiting his ailing mother at a nursing home in Jay, Okla., Mantle visited Smith's insurance office in nearby Quapaw. "Mickey had

Mickey doing a promotion for the Claridge Casino in Atlantic City, December '84.

gone into the bathroom and these people had spotted him from across the street," Corinne recalled. "They started coming toward the office and I told Mashall, 'Oh, goodness. They're coming in here for an autograph. Go stop them. This isn't a good time.'"

Another bathroom. What was it with Mantle, bathrooms and signatures? For Mantle, it was extremely difficult to find an autograph-free zone.

Mantle hated the entire aspect of autographs. "I could go over and over it with him, but up until the day he died, Mickey never understood why someone would want his autograph," Smith explained. "He would ask, 'Why do you think they make such a fuss over me like that?' I'd tell him, 'Because you look like an All-American boy. You've never lifted a weight in your life, but you have a 19 1/2-inch neck and they can hardly take your blood pressure because your forearms and arms are so solid. The speed and talent you have is something else. You play hard when you can hardly even walk. Plus you hit the ball a country mile. That's why they want your autograph.'"

Mantle called them "eyeballers."

"They would sit there and eyeball him while he was eating dinner or something," Smith said. "They'd come over and just about the time he was taking a bite, they'd say, 'Would you sign this?' Or, like I said before, when he went to the bathroom. It was awful hard for him just to go somewhere, even back home (in Commerce). That's

why when he came to visit we'd just drive around and stay in the car most of the time. I'd not let anyone know he was around.

"He couldn't go anywhere, really. He couldn't go to Six Flags. He couldn't go to a football game. He had to hide. He wished he could go in freedom just like everybody else. One time it was suggested that he wear a disguise. But Mickey said, 'Oh, no. If someone found out I did that ...' He didn't want a scandal or anything, no matter how small. He cared what people thought about him. He cared a great deal. He enjoyed being Mickey Mantle, but I don't think he liked having to hide. He was never more at ease than when he was on the golf course and in the clubhouse. People didn't bother him there."

Although a section of Smith's house is engulfed in Mantle memorabilia, much of it autographed, nearly every signature came unsolicited from Mantle. They were not requested.

And yet, other than Upper Deck (a trading card company which had Mantle under contract), perhaps no one asked Mantle for more autographs than Smith. He was the autograph hounds' liaison. Photographs, posters, sketches, drawings, baseballs, hats, gloves, bats, T-shirts, magazines, programs, pennants, blank pieces of paper -- you name it and Smith requested it. And it wasn't easy. Smith wasn't too keen on the autograph craze himself.

"Mickey told somebody else that he felt sorry for me because so many people went through me

Greer Johnson and Craig Stadler at Shangri-La in '93

Mantle sulked in guilt.

"What really stressed him out was when he would treat kids badly when they tried to get his autograph," Smith said. "He'd say 'no' and it bothered him when he did. He kept adding to his drinking. It hurt him. He'd say something to someone later. He'd say, 'Why'd I do that? Do you think I upset them?' That would really bother him. It bothered him his whole life."

For a solid decade before his death, Mantle often preached publicly for kids to stay away from alcohol and not use him as a role model. Do as I say, not as I do. The fact this message came from a drunk destroyed its credibility.

In the mid-1980s, Mantle was battling blinding headaches and wild anxiety attacks. Without warning, he would hyperventilate and shake, which was brought on by his heavy drinking, which was brought on by his remorse, which often was brought on by the unrelenting attention from the public, who almost always wanted his John Hancock. It was an endless cycle. The drinking stopped after his 1994 stay at the Betty Ford Center. The autograph demands, however, never stopped.

Not everyone was guilty.

"A lot of teammates wouldn't bother Mickey for his autograph," Smith said. "Billy (Martin) and Yogi (Berra) wouldn't ask him, but they sure as hell would ask me. He was always in such great demand compared to other players. Yogi once told

for autographs," Smith said. "A lot of times it was rather awkward. It didn't make any difference to me, really. Hey, it was an honor."

Many times the autograph seekers sought a little too hard. They were rude, intrusive and persistent. It wasn't always "Sign here, please." Sometimes it was "Here, sign this" or "Hey, Mick" followed by the particular item of the moment being shoved into his face. Sometimes no words would be spoken at all, just an implied demand.

And when that demand wasn't met, often

Corinne and Marshall join Mickey at the autograph table during his '92 golf tournament.

me 'If I sign one autograph, Mickey signs 10,000.' Once Mickey starts, he can't quit."

During idle moments, Mantle would sign the hand-sized photograph he handed out by the thousands. He'd go to the bathroom (yes, again the bathroom) and sign whatever he felt needed to be signed. If Mantle signed now, he wouldn't have to sign (as much) whenever the next barrage began.

"He had autograph signing down to a science," said former standout running back Steve Owens. "I never asked him for an autograph ..."

A smile then crept onto Owens' face as he admitted, "I had somebody else do it, usually Marshall or (Smith's wife) Corinne. But because I

knew him, people always asked me to get his autograph. One time when we went to the condo at Shangri-La, we had Corinne in the back of the car and you couldn't hardly see her. There were bats and balls and pictures and stuff. Marshall and I asked her, 'Would you have him sign all this stuff? We don't want to ask him.' Two hours later, she was back and he had signed everything.

"There was another time I came in with a bunch of stuff and four bats. Mickey said, 'I don't sign bats. I have this contract with Upper Deck and I'm not supposed to sign bats.' I said, 'That's OK. Don't worry about it. Sign what you want.' He was so meticulous when he signed those base-

Mickey signing a bat for the charity aution at the '93 golf tournament. The bat was auctioned off for $8,200.00.

balls. Again he said, 'I don't sign bats.' I said, 'Forget it, don't worry about it.' We talked a few minutes longer, he stopped in mid-sentence, paused and said, 'Ah, give me those damn bats.' For his friends, Mickey just couldn't say no."

Mantle once produced a huge photo he had kept between a mattress and box spring. It was of the final home run of his career, No. 536, which he hit on Sept. 20, 1968. The enscription: "To Steve: My favorite Okie. Mickey Mantle."

"Boy, do I treasure it," Owens said.

Owens also witnessed the dark side to the Mantle autograph phenomenon. "One time, I saw him refuse to sign a kid's autograph," Owens recalled. "As young as I was at the time, I think I was 23 or 24 (playing for the Detroit Lions), I didn't understand it. That's the one time I was bothered by it. But as I got to know him, I understood. People were just on top of him all the time. I'll never forget one lady who walked up to him at a charity golf tournament with about six baseballs. Mickey signed them, but you could tell by his face the whole fun of the evening had been drained out of him."

Barry Switzer, the former University of Oklahoma coach, now with the Dallas Cowboys, and Owens are good friends. Both men have signed more than a few autographs themselves.

"There was one time Mickey was sitting there all by himself, signing autographs," Owens said. "Barry shook his head, leaned over to me and said

Greer Johnson helps Mickey autograph baseballs at the 15th hole of his '94 golf tournament.

something like, 'It must be really tough to be a super-hero.' But that's what Mickey was. Some people, you can tell, were scared to ask for his autograph. I think his reputation got out about him jumping on people."

"There's not many people in the same league as Mickey when it came to signing autographs. Michael Jordan, maybe Troy Aikman. Most of us don't even come close. I'm happy to sign autographs whenever I'm asked. I'm flattered. But to think you could never go to a mall, or movie, or even the bathroom. That has to be tough. That rarely happened with me. Nowhere close."

Mike Samara, who managed the Mickey Mantle Holiday Inn Hotel in Joplin, Mo., said, "Mickey gave me an autographed picture of himself right after he won the Triple Crown (in 1956), when we were starting a business together. I said, 'Keep your damn picture. What the hell am I gonna do with this?'"

The 72-year-old Samara shared the story as he produced a well-protected item from an aged folder. You couldn't wipe the smile off Samara's face. The photograph he had no interest in keeping had remained a prized possession for 40 years.

"If you had Bob Hope, Elizabeth Taylor, Gregory Peck or any of those big stars at an autograph show, they might have 1,000 people waiting in line for an autograph. Mickey would have 10,000," Smith said. "Mickey once told me he signed something like 350 autographs in an hour. And he worked hard on his signature so everybody could read it."

Dr. J. Frederick McNeer, the specialist from the Warren Clinic in Tulsa who initially diagnosed Mantle's Type C hepatitis in September of 1994, was on the phone during one of Mantle's visits. Mantle picked up a softball that was on McNeer's desk, a ball that had been autographed by a third-grade softball team McNeer had helped coach. "Thanks Doc: Mickey Mantle" was the freshly scrolled message.

There was always a crowd of autograph seekers for Mickey.

Darrell Royal, Marshall Smith and Mickey at Shangri-La Golf Tournament in '94.

"I'm telling you, I would never part with that," McNeer said. "He had a unique signature. I like it."

When the exam was done, Mantle brought in roughly a dozen limited edition trading cards and autographed them. "He said I was the only doctor here who hadn't asked for his autograph," an appreciative McNeer said. "I said, 'You didn't come here for me to ask for an autograph. You came here for me to examine you.' My daughter, Meghan, has two cards that are almost hermetically sealed. Back then, she just thought that was the most amazing thing to have those autographs from Mickey Mantle."

The Smith's oldest daughter, Corinne, had known Mantle her entire life. She didn't get her first autograph until she was 28.

During one of Mantle's final visits to Commerce, he and Smith stopped at a photo shop to get some film processed. "I'll give you $20 if you can do this in 30 minutes," Mantle told the woman working behind the counter. She responded with, "I don't want the $20. If you give me an autograph, I'd be glad to do it for you."

Mantle waited in Smith's living room while the photos were developed. Uncertain what to do for the woman behind the counter, Mantle spotted one his favorite photos that Corinne had mounted on the wall. Mantle took the picture out of its frame, signed it and gave it to the woman. Mantle then returned to the Smith house and autographed the glass cover of the now-empty picture frame. "Thanks a lot Corinne," it read.

"Mickey would get the urge to do stuff like that all the time," Marshall Smith said. "You didn't ask him. He just did it. He felt good about it, too."

Mantle would visit his mother at a nursing home in Jay. Lovell Mantle had Alzheimer's disease -- a brain disorder which causes mood

Yogi Berra and Mickey in '92 at Shagri-La.

Mickey, Chris Stadler and Craig Stadler at the Shangri-La Golf Tournament. October '93.

Mickey with Stan "The Man" Musial doing the old "Spoon on Nose" trick.

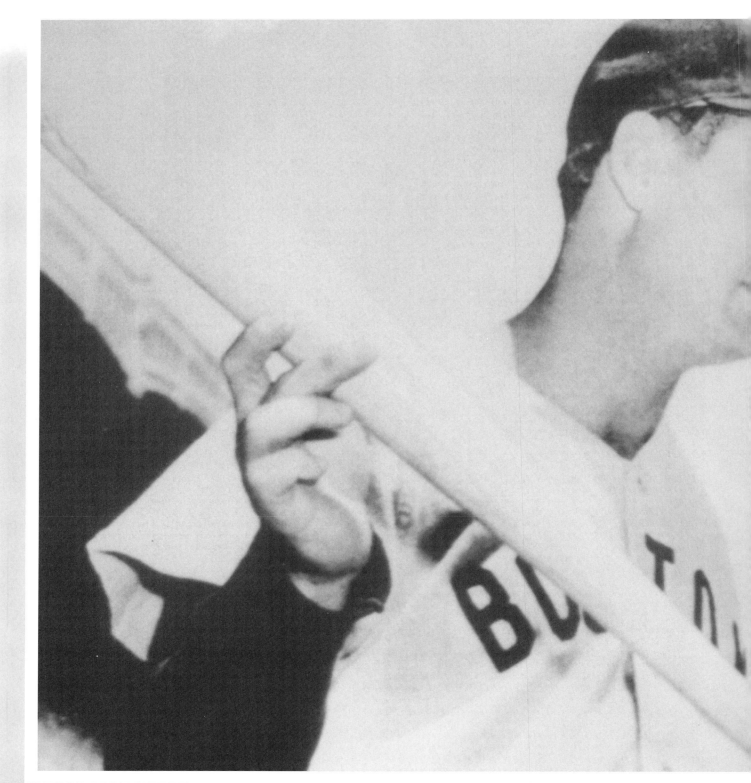

Ted Williams and Mickey at the beginning of Mickey's career with the Yankees.

Mickey with his mom and Marshall Smith at the nursing home in Jay, Oaklahoma. December '93.

changes, memory lapses, and time and spatial dis-orientation. Mantle's mother often couldn't remember her son's name.

"Late in her life, Mickey would say, 'I just wish she'd go ahead and die. It's too painful to deal with," Smith said. "Mickey never wanted to go to the nursing home alone. Someone, either me or Corinne, always went with him."

Lovell usually could be found in the TV room. On good days, she'd recognize her Hall of Famer and flash a smile. Mantle's visits caused a ruckus among the elderly.

"Next thing you know, there's six or seven people there asking him for his autograph," Smith said. "Mick would say, 'Do you mind if I sit here and visit with my mother? I'll leave some auto-graphs at the front desk.' When we got ready to go, Mickey would say, 'Corinne, would you mind going out to the glove box in the car and get those cards?' Corinne would come back with a handful and Mickey would say, 'Momma, here's some pic-tures you can give out to to the people you like.' Mickey always said to do that -- 'Hand them out to the people you like.'"

Mantle always bought his mother a dozen roses or nice flowers. "On the card he'd sign, 'I love you mom. Mick,'" Smith said. "We used to watch and see how quick that card would disap-pear because somebody wanted his autograph. It didn't take long, either. It was usually gone within five minutes."

Little Mickey and Big Mickey in '94

It was this association with autograph seekers which left behind arguably the best Mantle tale of all. In 1987, on the 20th anniversary of his 500th home run, Mantle told a USA Today reporter one of his favorites:

"You know, I dreamed I died, and when I got up to heaven, St. Peter met me at the pearly gates and said I couldn't get in because I hadn't always been good." Mantle said. " 'But before you go,' St. Peter said, 'God has six dozen baseball's He'd like you to sign.'"

Chances are good, wherever Mickey Mantle is right now, he's signing autographs.

LOSING A LEGEND

Mickey Mantle's final chapter, but the legend lives on.

The courage he displayed wearing hospital garb matched the courage he displayed while in uniform. Both performances were overwhelmingly impressive, undeniably memorable.

"He wore those Yankee pinstripes with honor," Marshall Smith said. "It was like watching the American flag go by."

Doctors who treated Mantle shortly before his death used "tough," "brave" and "a fighter" to describe him as a patient.

The state of Oklahoma has an impressive array of native celebrities. They include humorist Will Rogers, legendary athlete Jim Thorpe, Olympic gymnast Shannon Miller, film writer/producer Blake Edwards, singers Patti Page, Woodie Guthrie and Leon Russell, plus many personalities including Ben Johnson, Dale Robertson, James Garner, Tony Randall, Chuck

Part of the Mickey Mantle monument at Shangri-La.

Norris, Ron Howard, Ed Harris, Vera Miles, Alfred Woodard and Rue McClanahan.

The country music field is overflowing with folk born inside state lines -- Vince Gill, Reba McEntire, Garth Brooks, Toby Keith, Joe Diffie, Hoyt Axton, Brooks and Dunn, and many others.

Oklahoma is well-represented in baseball. There is Johnny Bench of Binger, Paul and Lloyd Waner of Harrah, Pepper Martin of McAlester, Ralph Terry of Big Cabin, Johnny Ray of Chouteau, U.L. Washington of Stringtown, plus Allie Reynolds, Bobby Murcer, Joe Carter, Darrell Porter and Mickey Tettleton from Oklahoma City. Willie Stargell of Earlsboro and Alvin Dark of Comanche were born in Oklahoma, but moved away at a young age. Warren Spahn (Buffalo, N.Y.), Carl Hubbell (Carthage, Mo.), Ferguson Jenkins (Ontario, Canada) and Bill Russell (Pittsburg, Kan.) moved to Oklahoma during or after their careers.

Other than Will Rogers and Jim Thorpe, perhaps no Oklahoma native was more widely

Spring Training, 1956.

revered than Mickey Mantle. He was immediately associated with his home state, an identifiable source of pride.

"He meant everything to me," Bench said of Mantle. "I wanted to wear No. 7 and play center field just like him. But all I could do is wear No. 7, because I sure couldn't play center field."

"Mickey was bigger than life to me," Murcer said. "Even though he was a superstar, he was still a genuine, good-hearted person. And if he was a friend, he was your friend for life."

While Mantle was supposed to become the next DiMaggio, former Yankees Tom Tresh and Murcer were supposed to become the next Mantle.

Like Mantle, Tresh was a switch-hitter with power and an erratic shortstop who likely would be moved to the outfield. The fact that Murcer also was an Oklahoma native and found the major leagues at the same age as Mantle (19) added fuel to that fire.

"It was extremely flattering." Murcer said of the comparisons to Mantle, "but not taken to heart."

Tresh failed the rather impossible feat of becoming the next Mantle. The fact is, there won't ever be another Mantle.

> "*He meant everthing to me,*" Bench said of Mantle. "*I wanted to wear No. 7 and play center field just like him*

In the book *The Last Hero*, Tresh said, "When I was a kid, I used to go to Tigers' Stadium and sit in the center-field bleachers and watch him play. In high school, I kind of mimicked everything he did, mimicked his run, the way he hit. I was a switch-hitter, and I watched how Mickey stood at the plate, his mannerisms, everything. If you look at some of my (153) home runs when I was playing for the Yankees (1960-69), if you look at the footage of me running around the bases, I probably went around a little faster than he did, but I also kinda tilted my head like he did. I have a son named Mickey. When he was born, he weighed 7 pounds, 7 ounces, and he was born on the 19th of October. Mickey Mantle's birthday is October 20th. I told my wife, if you could just bear down a little bit, if you could just hold on another 16 hours, we'd hit his birthday, you know?"

Murcer also entered the majors as a shortstop. When Murcer was inducted into the Oklahoma Sports Hall of Fame in 1993, Mantle gave the introduction. "The first time I ever heard of Bobby Murcer, they said a kid from Oklahoma was gonna be the next Mickey Mantle. They were right. Sure enough, he couldn't play shortstop, either."

Although he had a solid 17-year career with the Yankees, Giants and Cubs, Murcer also fell

Mickey talking to a crowd at his '93 Golf Tournament

short of Mantle's standards with a .277 lifetime batting average and 252 home runs in 1,908 games. Murcer was, however, one of the all-time Yankee favorites. On June 20, 1983, he retired. On August 7, 1983, the Yankees organization celebrated Bobby Murcer Day.

Asked to categorize his relationship with Mantle, Murcer said, "I would say we were definitely friends, and fairly close at that. In the beginning, when I came to the Yankees (in 1965), the thing I remember most was his acceptance of me as a 19-year-old kid. Mickey doing that for me basically told everyone else to keep their hands off. I'm not sure why he did it, if it was because I was from Oklahoma or not. But I think he did it because he's just a good person."

When Smith and Mantle would go out to eat, they'd often pick one of their favorite restaurants with a private booth in the back, away from anyone's line of sight. Inevitably, Mantle would be spotted.

"There were so many times well-dressed, polite people would come up to Mickey," Smith said. "They weren't always looking for an autograph. A lot of them would come up and say, 'Mr. Mantle, I just want to shake your hand. You made it possible for me to go to the Betty Ford Center and cure my problem. The only reason I did it was because of you.' Mickey got that a lot. He never realized he had a hangover until he quit drinking. He once told me, 'I believe I had a hangover for more than 30 years.'"

Most times, there was only one way Mantle knew how to drink -- in excess.

During one card show appearance in Atlanta, Mantle began the day around 2 p.m. by drinking 3-4 bottles of red wine in roughly three hours. He was signing autographs and was fun to be around. Then came a sitdown dinner, with vodka as the main course, more autographs and more vodka. Around 8 p.m., he emceed a banquet.

Mickey got that a lot. He never realized he had a hangover until he quit drinking

Despite all the pre-banquet activity, Mantle surprisingly kept his composure. Later, as usual, he remembered nothing.

In 1991, Smith helped take charge of Mantle's Make-A-Wish charity golf tournament. Promptly the tournament was moved from the 18-hole facility at Loma Linda, in Joplin, Mo., to the 36-hole Shangri-La Resort in Afton, Okla.

The three-day event would call for Mantle to be stationed at a par-3 hole each day. He would play the hole and pose with each group that played through. He'd also take on just about any financial proposition. People would bet X amount that Mantle's tee-shot would end up farther away from the hole than theirs. All in the name of charity, mind you.

"By the time my group got to that par-3, it was late in the evening," Steve Owens recalled. "All that was left on the tee box was that old snake Mickey used to scare people, and about six empty bottles of wine. That's it. Mick wasn't there anymore. Everybody would be saying, 'Hey we're coming up on the hole where we get to challenge The Mick.' Then when we got there, he was long gone."

"But the next day, Mickey searched for any groups he might have missed and had his picture taken with them," Smith said.

Owens worked several charities alongside Mantle.

"Mickey was never presumptuous," Owens said. "I never saw him act that way, like people owed him special treatment. In fact, I thought he was always the opposite. He liked it when you didn't treat him like Mickey Mantle. That's what (Owens' wife) Barbara did. She didn't give a damn that he was Mickey Mantle or whoever, and

Tom Tresh, Hank Bauer, Moose Skowron, and Yogi Berra at the Mantle Monument, Shangri-La Resort in Afton, Oklahoma.

Roy Clark singing "Yesterday" to Mickey at his '94 Golf Tournament.

they got along great.

"Mickey was extremely humble. He got short with people and his frustrations came out when he drank. His emotions really came out then. I always thought he cared about people, though. He'd come up to me after a benefit and say, 'Hey, thanks for your help.' He always said that. He'd almost mumble it, as though he was apologizing that he asked you to do it."

An astounding 450 golfers signed up for the first Mantle tournaments at Shangri-La, and that number has remained steady. "It was a party, I'll tell you that," Smith said.

Though Mantle is gone, the tournament will continue. It is now sponsored by the Heisman Memorial Trophy Trust, bearing the new title: The Heisman Salutes Oklahoma Youth -- Keeping the youth's Dream Alive.

Evidently, lawyers representing Merlyn Mantle are upset with the ongoing use of Mantle's name.

"We're going to try to continue what Mick wanted us to do.," Owens said, ignoring threats from the lawyers. "What are you gonna do, come after us? Shut us down in the name of charity because we use the name Mick? Hey, there's a lot of guys named Mick out there."

"We're talkin' about Mick Thompson," Smith deadpanned. "You mean, you don't know Mick

Thompson?"

"That's right," Owens said, "and we're just keeping Mick's dream alive."

Owens never did get to play golf with Mantle. "Steve constantly was reminded he 'wasn't good enough to play with a Hall of Famer,' " Smith said. "So when I first saw Mickey after his liver transplant, he was weak and could barely talk. I relayed a message from Steve."

Smith: "Steve said to tell you he's ready for you. He think's he finally can take you at golf."

Mickey: "Don't make me laugh. It hurts when I laugh."

Shortly after the liver transplant, Mantle told Smith he had planned on getting a house at Shangri-La. "He wanted to live up here. He loved it here." Smith said. "And the first thing he wanted to do was get a boat like Steve's (a 28-foot cruiser). He kept saying he wanted to get a little bigger boat than Steve's. He always wanted to outdo Steve just a little bit."

How much bigger? Two feet? One foot?

"No, one inch," Owens replied. "It was a compulsion with him, but in a kidding way."

"Mickey was proud of Steve," Smith said.

To close friends, Mantle would talk golf. To friendly acquaintances, he'd talk baseball. And when Mantle was drunk, well, he'd just plain talk.

"I'll never forget going down to the Road

Evidently, lawyers representing Merlyn Mantle are upset with the ongoing use of Mantle's name

194

House (a restaurant near Shangri-La)," Owens said. "Mickey, Hank, Moose, Yogi, Bob Costas and (Mantle's boyhood idol) Stan Musial were all there. That's when Mickey was still drinking and he got tanked. When he got tanked, he held court. It just got crazy. It was fortunate we had a private room because of the language that was being used."

Mantle's primary distractions were drinking, golfing and gambling. It's somewhat miraculous Mantle didn't relocate to Las Vegas at some point in his life.

"He loved to gamble," Owens said. "He used to call me and say, 'Do you think Dallas will cover?' I'd tell him, 'Hell, Mickey, I don't know. I don't bet.' He'd say, 'Well, I just put $1,000 on Dallas ... So, do you think they'll cover?' He'd just keep proddin'."

The constant drinking also clouded Mantle's judgment. "He owned a home at Loma Linda, but he never had a key to the house," Smith said. "We'd always go up there, but he never had the key. It seemed like he never had a key to anything. He'd get mad and break the door down to get in."

Mantle: "Mott, if I don't find that key, I'm gonna break the damn door down."

Smith: "Don't do that. You've got a telephone outside. Just call a locksmith."

"The guy was there, I'll bet you, within 10 minutes and it took about one second to get the door unlocked. It cost something like $20," Smith said. "Mick said, 'I wonder why I never thought about that? It cost us thousands of dollars to get all these damn doors fixed.'"

In 1994, which would be his final appearance at the Make-A-Wish charity tournament, a frustrated Mantle approached Smith shortly before giving his annual speech. At the time, Mantle was in his 10th month of sobriety.

Mantle: "What should I say, Mott? What should I tell them?"

Smith: "Just tell them what you tell them every year."

Mantle: "What's that?"

Smith: "You know. Thank them all for coming and that you're happy they could all make it. Congratulate all the celebrities. That sort of thing."

Mantle: "That's what I always tell them?"

"He had absolutely no idea what he said at all those other banquets," Smith said. "He had been so drunk most of the time, he didn't remember a thing. But when he got up there ... man, the speech he gave would have ripped your heart out. That was really the beginning of him being strong for himself. From that day forward."

Mantle's impromptu effort was greeted with tears and a standing ovation.

When Mantle would watch old footage of himself, especially from the 1950s, he admitted he couldn't remember playing. "It's like it's somebody else," Mantle often said. "I mean, it's not like it's me, you know. I can hardly remember it."

These lapses in memory helped push Mantle toward the Betty Ford Center and to Dr. J. Frederick McNeer, the man who initially discovered Type C hepatitis in Mantle. Sheer willpower, McNeer said, is what made Mantle's trip to the clinic a success.

"He was having withdrawals," McNeer said of Mantle's temporary escape from Betty Ford when he snuck out, purchased a beer and did nothing but stare at it. "That kind of strength is not intellectual or emotional. It must have been tremendously painful for Mickey not to drink that beer."

Mantle was an incredibly charitable man.

Too sick to play but still wanting to do his part in April of 1995, Mantle signed autographs for two full days at a golf benefit held by Ben Crenshaw, Willie Nelson and Darrell Royal at Barton Creek in Austin, Texas. Just 12 days prior, Crenshaw had won his second Masters tournament.

The charity golf classic raised $15,000, which promptly was matched by a Texas millionaire. The Mickey Mantle Warren Foundation also chipped in $10,000. The $40,000 was donated to victims of the Oklahoma City bombing, which killed 168 people and injured hundreds of others. The bombing occurred April 19, just two days before the charity event.

Listed on the back of the 1996 Shangri-La tournament brochure were 19 beneficiaries, including the American Cancer Society, the Bill Mantle Fund and the Roger Maris Cancer Fund.

When it came to dealing with death, Mantle struggled. He struggled badly. He and Maris had a much closer friendship after they had retired than while they were playing. Maris' death in 1985 hit Mantle hard, as did Billy Martin's unexpected death four years later. The early departures from the Mantle family tree were devastating.

"Billy's death tore him up," Smith said. "At that time, Mickeys' drinking was as bad as I can remember."

"I rarely get close to people," Mantle once told Costas. "I'm weird, I guess. When I did drink too much, it somehow relieved the pressure of what I should have been."

And there was Mantle's lifelong reputation of being, well, not bright.

"Mickey was no dummy," Smith said several times. "We asked him to write a little note we can put into the tournament program. He pulled out a napkin and started writing."

This is what Mantle came up with: "I guess in all our lives we want to do something we could be proud of. I've been very lucky in mine -- but I am proud to be part of Make-A-Wish and I know you are, too. Thanks a lot."

Two months after Mantle's death, the cover of the Shangri-La Golf Classic program offered the following: "A hundred years from now it will not matter what my bank account was, the sort of house I lived in, or the kind of car I drove. But, the world may be different because I was important in the life of a child."

Said Smith, "Nobody had a warmer heart than the Mick when it came to kids. Mickey wrote his own scripts like that all the time."

In the final months of his life, Mantle turned to former teammate Bobby Richardson, a lay minister who lived in South Carolina. It was after having his liver transplant that Mantle told Richardson he had accepted Christ as his savior. They had several conversations via telephone and Richardson was in the pulpit during Mantle's funeral.

"I think Mickey always believed in God, I really do," Smith said. "He thought if he would do some things he didn't do before, maybe God would help him a little bit more. I think we all feel that way. I know as I get older, I look up there (heaven) more than I did when I was young -- I can tell you that, for sure. He does a lot for me today, and He did a lot for Mickey."

"There were four churches in Commerce," Mantle wrote. "I must've been in all of them at one time or another. Yet nobody in my family took religion seriously. I suppose it was dad's influence. He used to say, 'Religion doesn't necessarily make you good. As long as your heart is in the right place, and you don't hurt anyone, I think you'll go

No body had a warmer heart when it came to kids. Mickey wrote his own scripts like that all the time

to heaven -- if there is one.' Mom felt the same way. She backed him no matter what he believed."

A sober Mantle would battle with the acceptance of his past. A drunk Mantle battled loneliness.

"When I first retired (after the 1968 season), for about three or four years, it was kind of like, 'Where did Mickey go?' " Mantle said in a television interview with Tulsa's Becky Dixon. "All of a sudden, the bubble-gum craze started and for some reason or another, I'm more popular that I've ever been in my life. It was like nobody cared. You start realizing, 'What happened?' I go to these card shows and now I make more money in two days that I did playing ball for a whole year ($100,000 was his top salary). So, it's really flattering."

On July 11, 1995, Mantle stole baseball's spotlight during the All-Star break. Forty pounds lighter since his June 8 liver transplant, Mantle held court at Baylor University Medical Center in Dallas, roughly 20 miles away from where the game's finest would gather at the Ballpark in Arlington later that same night.

The question-and-answer session was a self-cleansing opportunity for a fragile Mantle, who pleaded to fans, particularly the young ones. "All you gotta do is look at me," Mantle said, not reaching his full potential as a player and a person. "What I want to do is get it across to kids not to drink or do drugs. I was lucky."

Trouble was, Mantle's admirable behavior shortly before his death was precisely what worshipers were looking for, what they needed.

Steve Garvey endured more than his share of hero worship during his 19-year career in the major leagues (1969-87). "Through the years, fans have gone to the hero and the role models, so to speak," Garvey said. "Back when I was growing up, 'hero' was a term used for someone you looked up to, admired. They were people who did natural, inspiring things on a regular basis. To many people, Mickey Mantle did that. I wasn't that close to him. That usually starts with family and with friends. From there, it's purely up the individual. I'm sure Mickey knew what his excesses were. He just had to come to terms with it."

Garvey was an 8-year-old batboy at spring training when he first met Mantle. "My dad drove a bus for Greyhound and he had a charter a couple of times with the Yankees," said Garvey, who lived in Tampa at the time. "I was a Mickey Mantle fan growing up. I was a Brooklyn Dodger fan and a Mickey Mantle fan, which was a rather odd combination. Subsequently, when I got to the majors I

> "*What I want to do is get it across to kids not to drink or do drugs. I was lucky*"

met Mickey at a variety of different events, from All-Star games to card shows. We always had a nice rapport. He was somebody I truly respected for his accomplishments."

"Mickey said, 'Don't be like me,' " McNeer recalled. "Actually, I'd want my kid to be just like Mickey Mantle. I wouldn't want him to drink, but it's probably not surprising for a man who came into the league under those circumstances. I can't conceive of the pressure he was under. It had to be hard to be sober in New York City when you're 19 and faced with the job of replacing Joe DiMaggio, playing for the Yankees, and living that lifestyle. It's impossible for us to comment on such things because we just don't know how it would feel.

"He was probably one of the most gifted athletes in any sport. He was a shy, humble guy who never wanted a lot of notoriety, it just kinda came to him. He was a nice man, very easy to take care of. He was a role model when he said, 'Yeah, I had a problem and should have acted on it sooner.' He was very candid. That's one thing I always admired about him in the final year. He was enjoying life. People liked him and respected him. He didn't try to misrepresent himself to anybody. I haven't met too many people who gave as much to what they loved as Mickey Mantle did to baseball.

He was a growing man and he continued to grow until the day he died."

Mantle's news conference was riveting.

"I want to start giving something back," Mantle said. "I've been so lucky my whole life. I owe so much to God and the American people, and especially Baylor University. I think they saved my life. I want to work with Baylor University on a donor program. Anything I can do, that's what I want to do."

There was an immediate heightened awareness in organ donations. Actually, overall interest skyrocketed. Before Mantle had his transplant, an organ bank in the Dallas area fielded about 15 calls per day. Shortly after Mantle's news conference, they fielded hundreds.

Mantle also tossed out more than his share of levity. Former Yankee teammate Yogi Berra called and allegedly told Mantle, "He was going to come to my funeral because he was afraid I wouldn't come to his."

Renowned sports collector Barry Halper was in the audience and wondered how the removed liver was. "I figured he probably bought it," Mantle quipped.

Although the possibility of playing golf was at least three months away, Mantle pointed at one of his doctors and said, "I can beat him right now."

As for donating his own organs, Mantle said, "I don't have anything good to give or I would leave it. Everything I've got is wore out."

Baylor officials estimated more than 20,000 cards and letters were received offering Mantle encouragement. "All the people who wrote ... I'll never be able to pay it all back," Mantle said. "As soon as I get more stable and get to feeling better, I'm gonna try."

"He handled the entire situation with a lot of dignity," Garvey said. "I think over the last year and a half, he made a tremendous contribution to society by coming out and admitting he had flaws and that he did abuse alcohol. Just that alone was a tremendous education for the youth and for the adults of this country. In the end, he more than atoned for the problems he had."

Mantle's funeral was held on August 15, 1995, two days after his death. Murcer was one of Mantle's six pallbearers, alongside Berra, Whitey Ford, Johnny Blanchard, Bill "Moose" Skowron and Hank Bauer.

"I didn't really expect to be a pallbearer," Murcer said. "To tell the truth, the first time I heard about it was on ESPN. (Wife) Kay and I spoke with Merlyn right after Mickey died, but she never really said anything about it. Of course, I was honored."

An overflow crowd of roughly 2,000 filled the Lovers Lane United Methodist Church in Dallas. Some of the dignitaries included Musial, Reggie Jackson, acting baseball commissioner Bud Selig, former Yankees teammate, Tony Kubek and Dr. Bobby Brown, football star Pat

Marshall Smith and Mickey fishing together at Shangri-La in '94.

Summerall and Yankees owner George Steinbrenner.

Smith recalled the funeral for Billy Martin, who died in a car wreck on Christmas in 1989. Mantle was seated with several teammates when he was waved over by Steinbrenner to sit between himself and former President Richard Nixon.

"Mickey said that really bothered him," Smith recalled. "He didn't like that fanfare. He was highly disappointed in that funeral. He said he didn't want to be there with Nixon and Steinbrenner. He wanted to be with the ballplayers. That's when he said, 'I just don't want any elaborate funeral. He wanted a simple, family graveside service.' "

Mantle's funeral would be anything but simple. It was on nation-wide television. Smith said he didn't mind, and believes the Mantle family felt the same way. "It gave everyone a chance to celebrate Mickey," Smith said. "If that's what Merlyn wanted to do, and I'm pretty sure it was, she had every right to do exactly that."

It was at a Shangri-La banquet where Mantle heard legendary guitarist Roy Clark sing "Yesterday When I Was Young." Clark, born in Meherrin, Va., is a longtime resident of Oklahoma.

Mickey Mantle monument at the Shangri-La resort.

It was then that Mantle requested Clark sing that same song at his funeral.

"A promise is a promise," Clark said at Mantle's funeral. "It just wasn't supposed to happen this soon."

Smith's evaluation of the service? "I walked out of that church feeling better than I had felt in a long time," said Smith, who lost 15 pounds that summer during Mantle's ailments. "I just felt it had been done with class. Mickey went out with such dignity and gave himself to the Lord. My love for him got stronger and stronger in the last five years or so. I just wish I would have realized it at the time."

One of the most gifted people ever to play baseball was gone, but he is hardly forgotten. "I think about him every day," Smith said. "So do a lot of people."

And what is Mickey doing right now?

"He hasn't made a putt in forever, and he hasn't made himself any money," Smith whispered. "I think he's up there looking down on us, waiting for me to join him. And when it's time for me to line up that final putt down here, I'll look up and ask, 'Hey, Mick. Help me read this one, will ya?'"

"SO LONG, MICK.
AND THANKS

Eulogy by Bob Costas

It occurs to me as we're all sitting here thinking of Mickey, he's probably somewhere getting an earful from Casey Stengal, and no doubt quite confused by now.

One of Mickey's fondest wishes was that he be remembered as a great teammate, to know that the men he played with thought well of him. But it was more than that. Moose and Whitey and Tony and Yogi and Bobby and Hank -- what a remarkable team you were. And the stories of the visits you guys made to Mickey's bedside the last few days were heartbreakingly tender. It meant everything to Mickey, as would the presence of so many baseball figures past and present here today.

I was honored to be asked to speak by the Mantle family today. I am not standing here as a broadcaster. Mel Allen is the eternal voice of the Yankees and that would be his place. And there are others here with a longer and deeper association with Mickey than mine. But I guess I'm here not so much to speak for myself as to simply represent the millions of baseball-loving kids who grew up in the '50s and '60s and for whom Mickey Mantle was baseball.

And more than that, he was a presence in our lives -- a fragile hero to whom we had an emotional attachment so strong and lasting that it defied logic. Mickey often said he didn't understand it -- this enduring connection and affection -- for men in their 40s and 50s, otherwise perfectly sensible, who went dry in the mouth and stammered like school boys in the presence of Mickey Mantle.

Maybe Mick was uncomfortable with it, not just because of his shyness, but because he was always too honest to regard himself as some kind of deity. But that was never really the point. In a very different time than today, the first baseball commissioner, Kenesaw Mountain Landis, said every boy builds a shrine to some baseball hero, and before that shrine, a candle always burns.

For a huge portion of my generation, Mickey Mantle was that baseball hero. And for reasons that no statistic, no dry recitation of facts can possibly capture, he was the most compelling baseball hero of our lifetime. And he was a symbol of baseball at a time when the game meant something to us that perhaps it no longer does.

F **or a huge portion of my generation, Mickey Mantle was that baseball hero**

Mickey Mantle had those dual qualities so seldom seen, exuding dynamism and excitement but at the same time, touching your heart -- flawed and wounded. We knew there was something poignant about Mickey Mantle before we knew what poignant meant. We didn't just root for him, we felt for him.

Long before any of us cracked a serious book, we knew something about mythology as we watched Mickey Mantle run out a home run through the lengthening shadows of a late Sunday afternoon at Yankee Stadium.

There was greatness in him, but vulnerability, too. He was our guy. When he was hot, we felt great. When he slumped or got hurt, we sagged a bit, too. We tried to crease our caps like him; kneel in an imaginary on-deck circle like him; run like him, head down, elbows up.

Billy Crystal is here today. Billy said that at his bar mitzvah, he spoke in an Oklahoma drawl. Billy's here today because he loved Mickey Mantle, and millions more who felt like him are here today in spirit as well.

It's been said that the truth is never pure and rarely simple. Mickey Mantle was too humble and honest to believe that the whole truth about him could be found on a Wheaties box or a baseball card. But the emotional truths of childhood have a power to transcend objective fact. They stay with us through all the years, withstanding the ambivalence that so often accompanies the experiences of adults.

That's why we can still recall the immediate tingle in the instant of recognition when a Mickey Mantle popped up in a pack of Topps bubble gum cards -- a treasure lodged between an Eli Grba and a Pumpsie Green.

That's why we smile today, recalling those October afternoons when we'd sneak a transister radio into a school to follow Mickey and the Yankees in the World Series. Or when I think of Mr. Tomasee, a very wise sixth-grade teacher who understood that the World Series was more important, at least for one day, than any school lesson could be. So he brought his black-and-white TV from home, plugged it in, and let us watch it right there in school through the flicker and the static. It was richer and more compelling than anything I've seen on a high-resolution, big-screen TV. Of course, the bad part, Bobby, was that Koufax

Moose Skowran, Mickey, Yogi Berra, Marshall Smith and Hank Bauer at Shangri-La in '94.

Bob Costas and Marshall Smith at the Shangri-La Golf Tournament, '93.

struck 15 of you guys out that day.

My phone's been ringing the past few weeks as Mickey fought for his life. I've heard from people I hadn't seen or talked to in years -- guys I played stickball with, even some guys who took Wiilie's side in those endless Mantle-Mays arguments. They're grown up now. They have their families. They're not even necessarily big baseball fans anymore. But they felt something hearing about Mickey, and they figured I did, too.

In the last year Mickey Mantle, always so hard on himself, finally came to accept and appreciate that distinction between a role model and a hero. The first, he often was not. The second, he always will be.

And in the end, people got it. And Mickey Mantle got from America something other than misplaced and mindless celebrity worship. He got something far more meaningful. He got love -- love for what he had been; love for what he made us feel; love for the humanity and sweetness that was always mixed in with the flaws and all the pain that wracked his body and his soul.

We wanted to tell him that it was OK, that what he had been was enough. We hoped he felt that Mutt Mantle would have understood and that Merlyn and the boys loved him.

And in the end something remarkable happened, the way it does for champions. Mickey Mantle rallied. His heart took over, and he had some innings as fine as any in 1956, or with his buddy, Roger, in 1961. But this time, he did it in the harsh and trying summer of '95. And what he did was stunning. The sheer grace of that ninth inning -- the humility, the sense of humor, the total absence of self pity, the simple eloquence and honesty of his pleas to others to take heed of his mistakes.

All of America watched in admiration. His doctors said he was, in many ways, the most remarkable patient they'd ever seen. His bravery, so stark and real, that even those used to seeing people in dire circumstances were moved by his example. Because of that example, organ donations are up dramatically all across America. A cautionary tale has been honestly told and perhaps will affect some lives for the better.

And our last memories of Mickey Mantle are as heroic as the first. None of us, Mickey included, would want to be held to account for every

moment of our lives. But how many of us can say that our best moments were as magnificent as his?

This is the cartoon from this morning's Dallas Morning News. Maybe some of you saw it. It got torn a little bit on the way from the hotel to here. There's a figure here, St. Peter I take it to be, with his arm around Mickey, that broad back and the number 7. He's holding his book to admissions. He says, "Kid, that was the most courageous ninth inning I''ve ever seen."

"Kid, that was the most courageous ninth inning I've ever seen"

It brings to mind a story Mickey liked to tell on himself and maybe some of you have heard it. He pictured himself at the pearly gates, met by St. Peter, who shook his head and said, "Mick, we checked the record. We know some of what went on. Sorry, we can't let you in. But before you go, God wants to know if you'd sign these six dozen baseballs."

Well, there are days when Mickey Mantle was so darn good that we kids would bet even God would want his autograph. But like the cartoon says, I don't think Mick needed to worry much about the other part.

I just hope God has a place for him where he can run again. Where he can play practical jokes on his teammates and smile that boyish smile, 'cause God knows, no one's perfect. And God knows there's something special about heroes.

So long, Mick. And thanks.

"Yesterday When I Was Young" '48, Independence, Kansas.